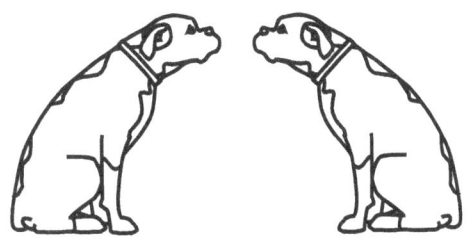

The Super Awesome Coloring Book

Featuring Original Artwork by Mark Cesarik

50 Super Awesome Designs
for the
Modern Coloring Enthusiast

The pages of this book are suitable for colored pencils,
markers, and a variety of other media.
To help prevent bleed-through, place a blank
sheet of paper between the pages when coloring.

for Cara & James

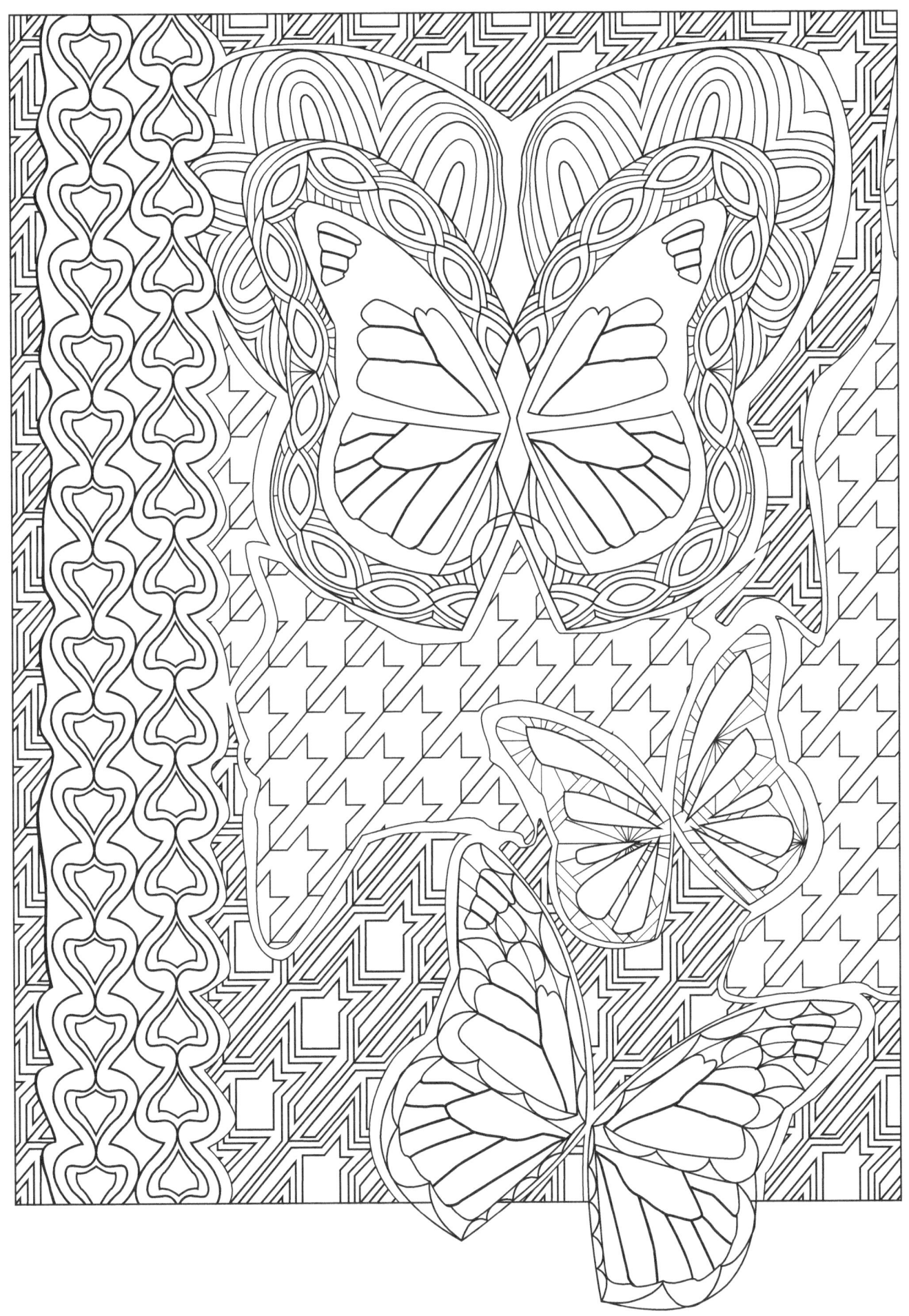

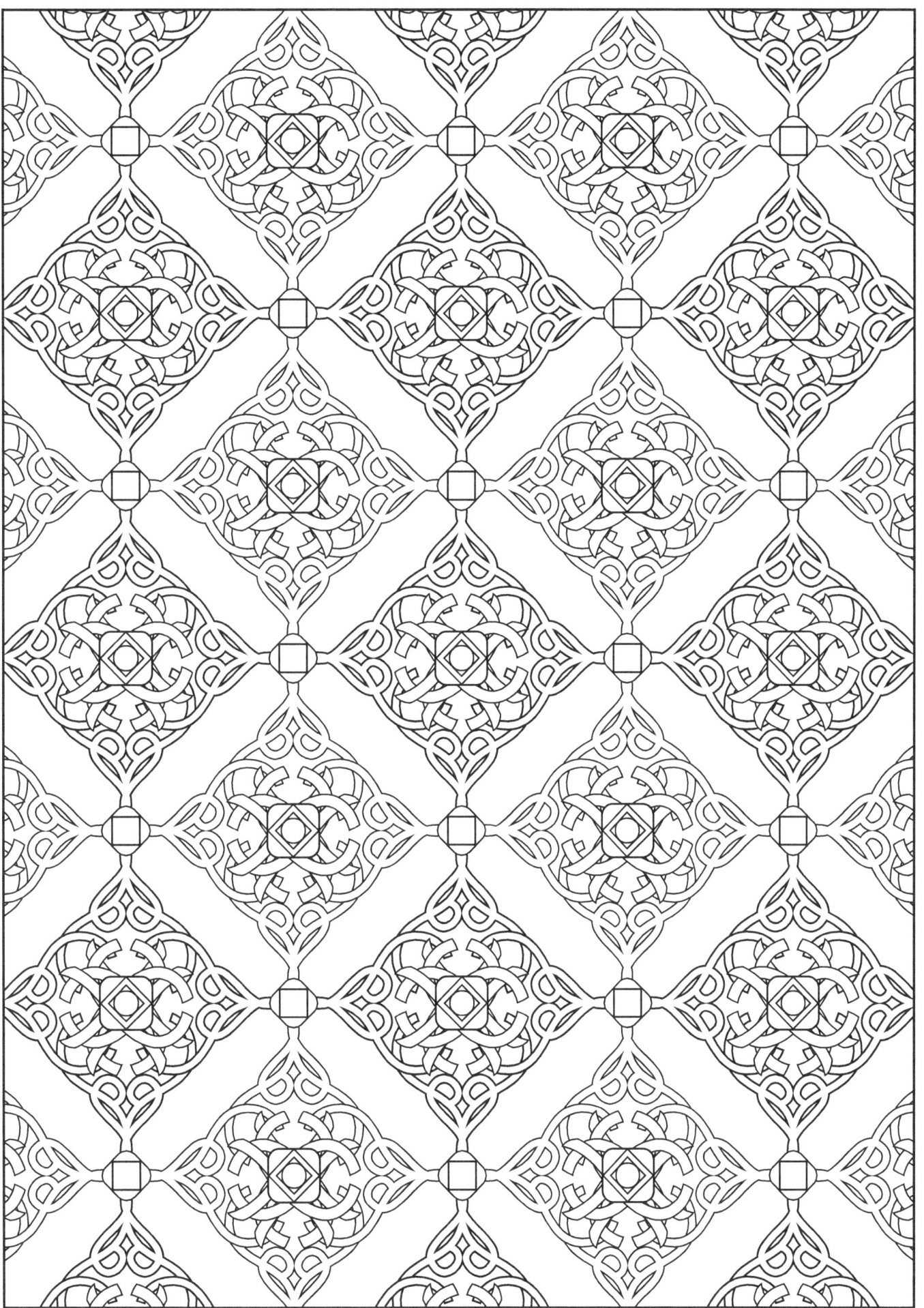

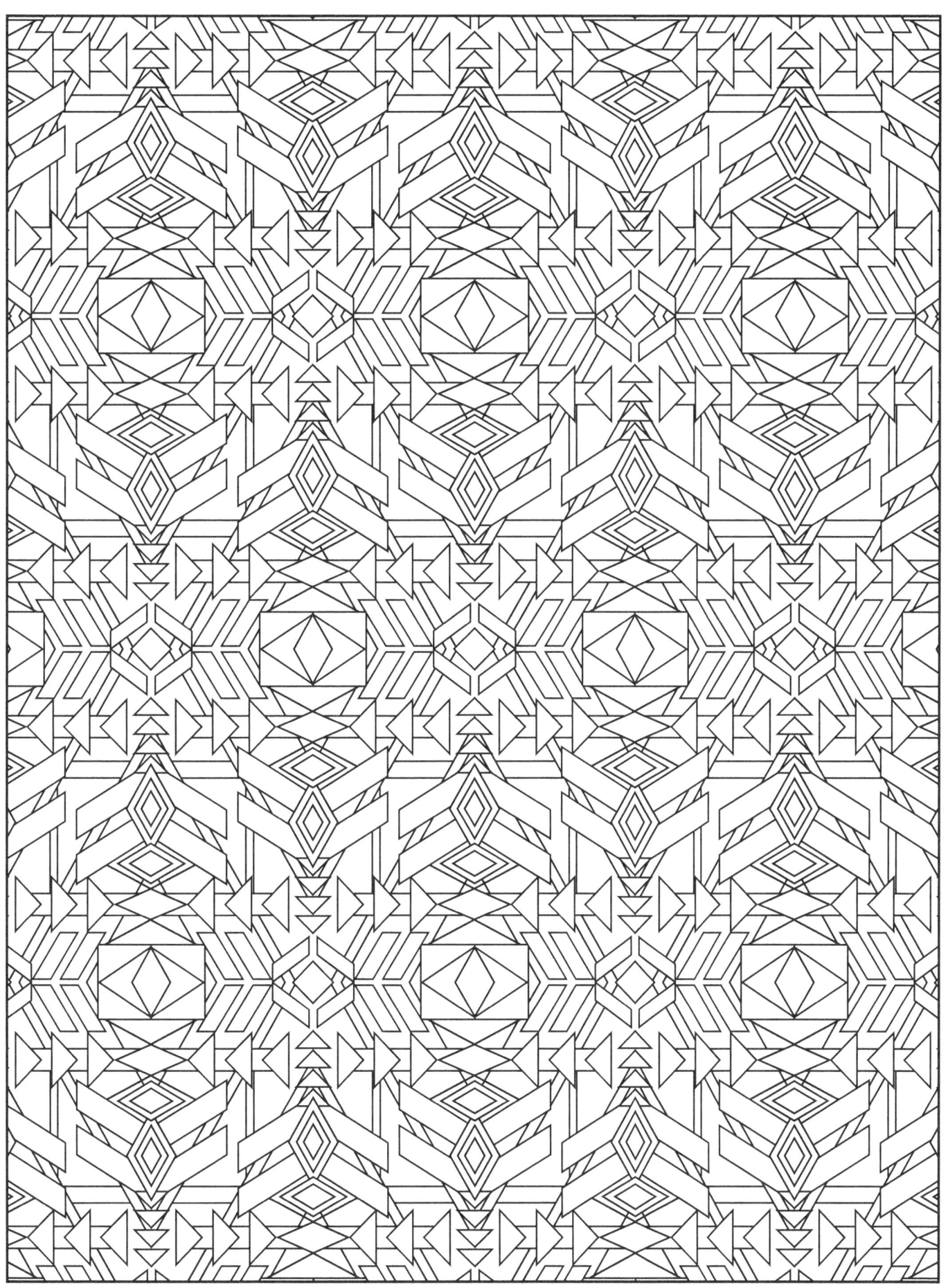

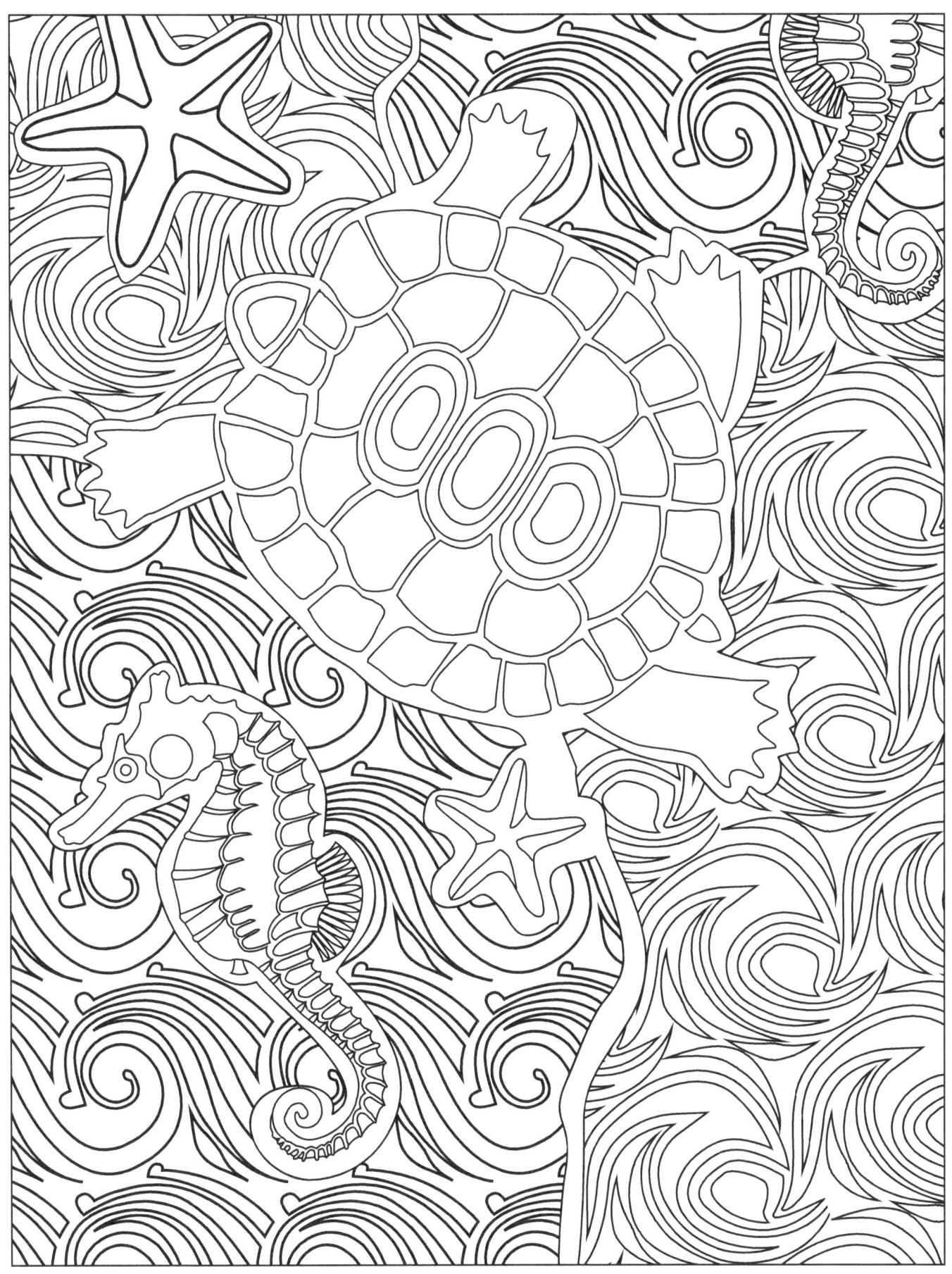

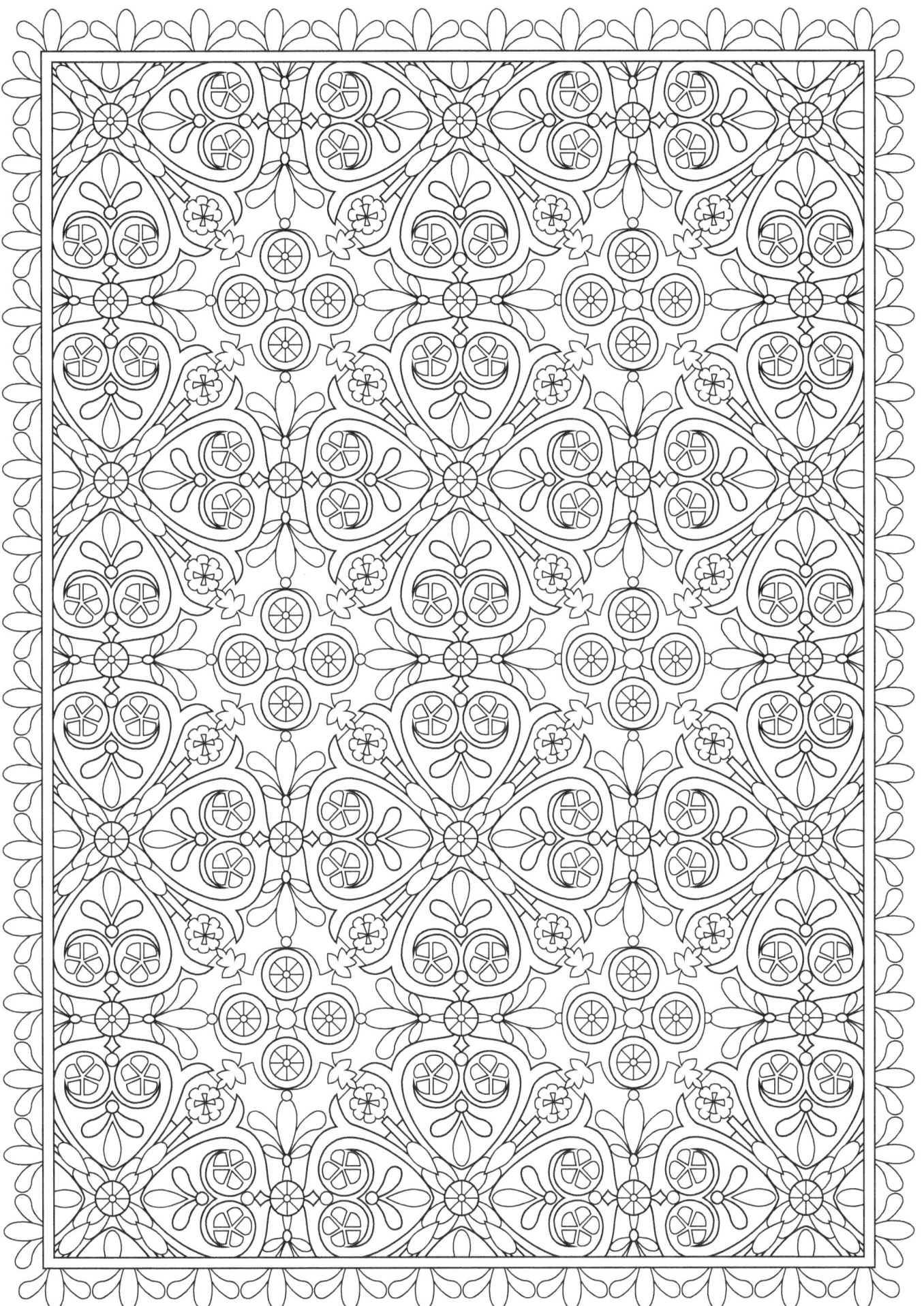

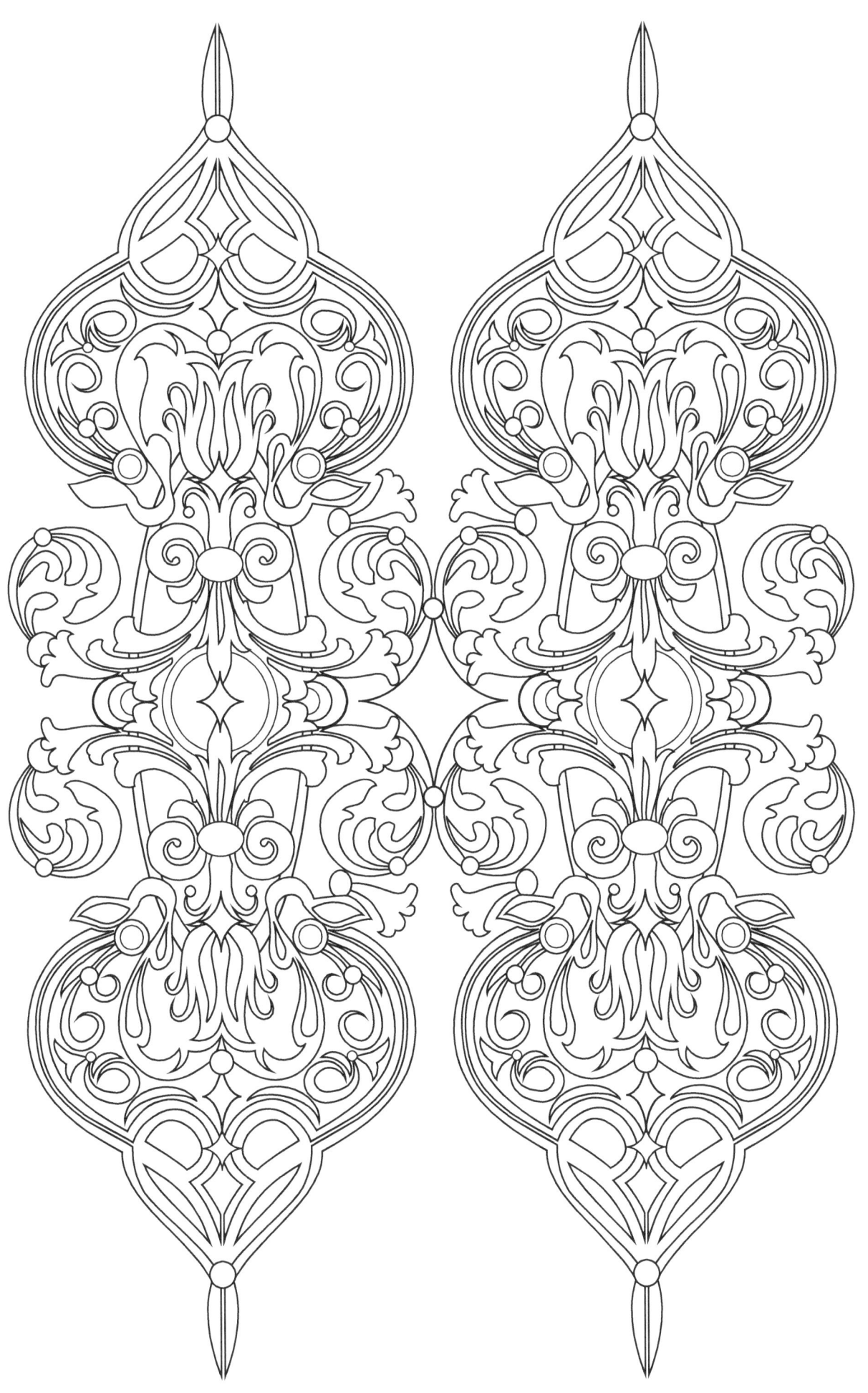

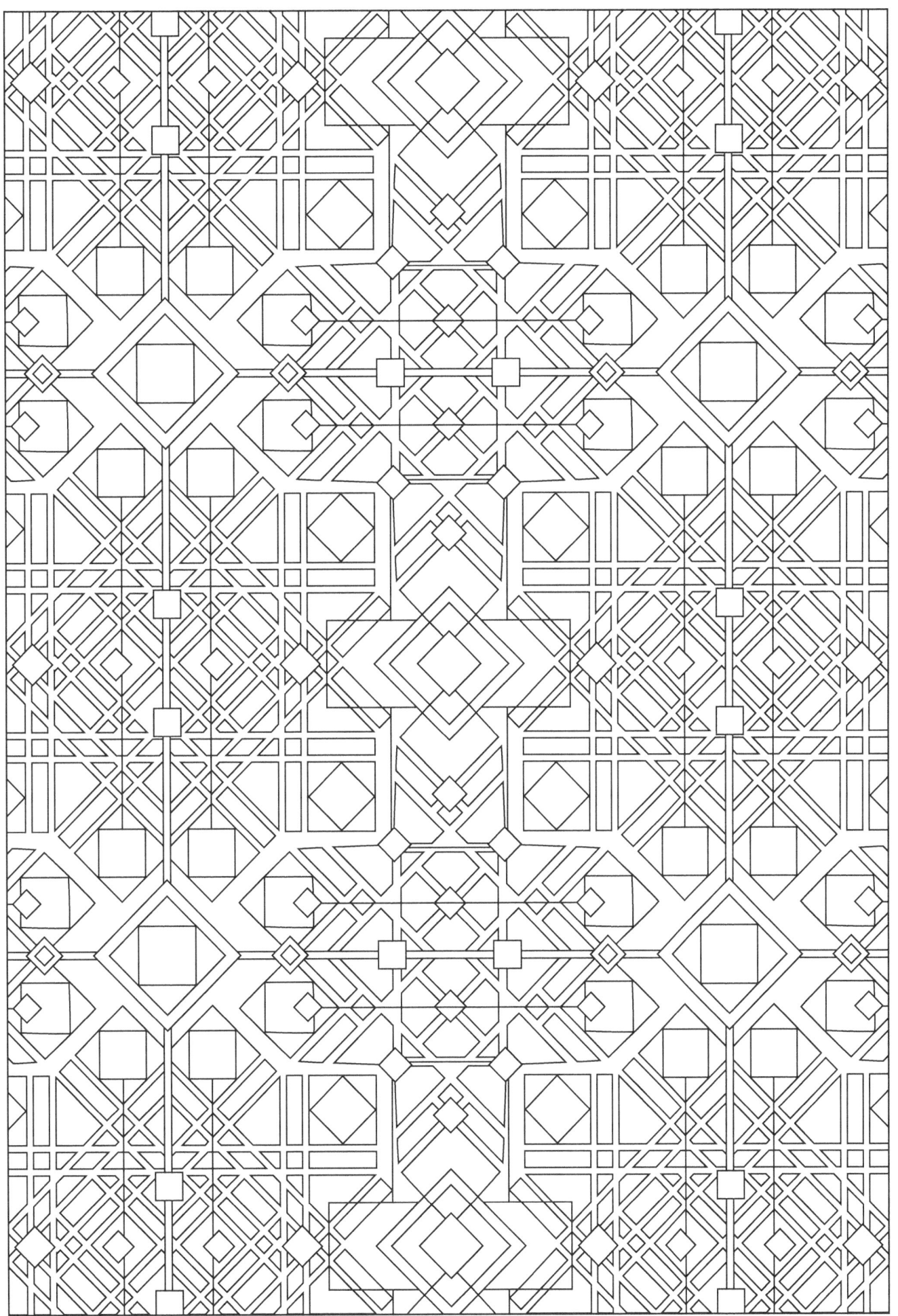

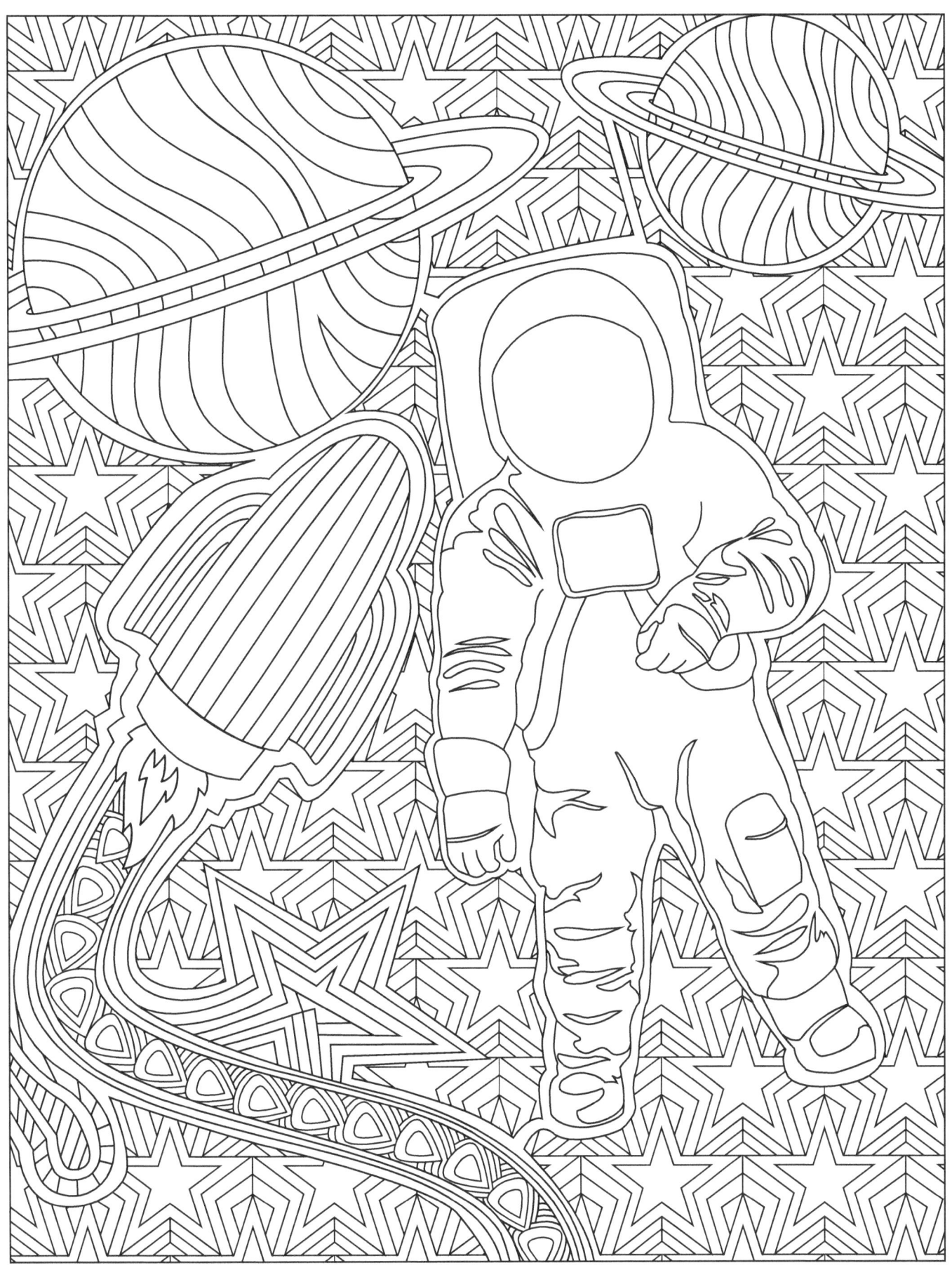

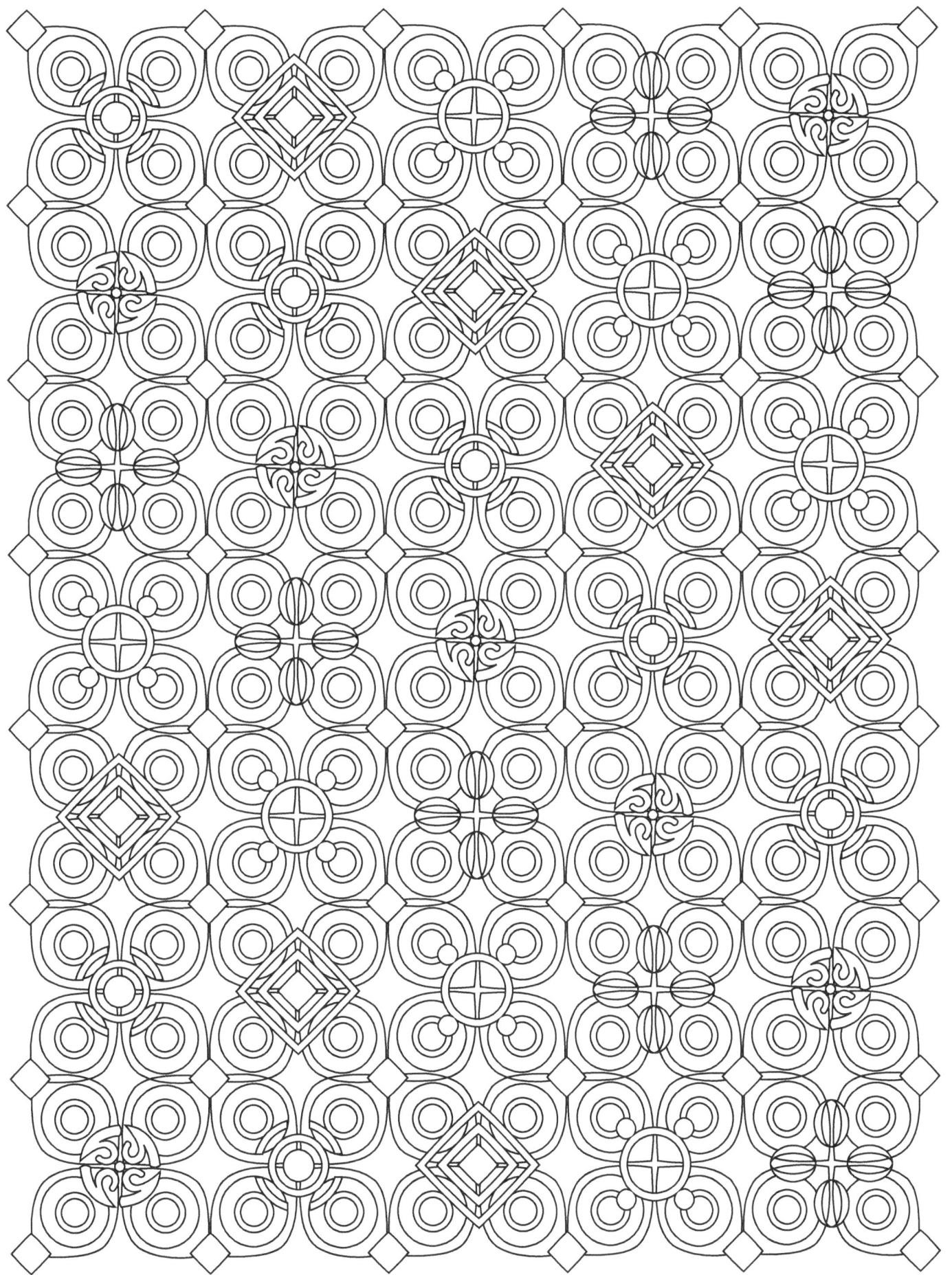

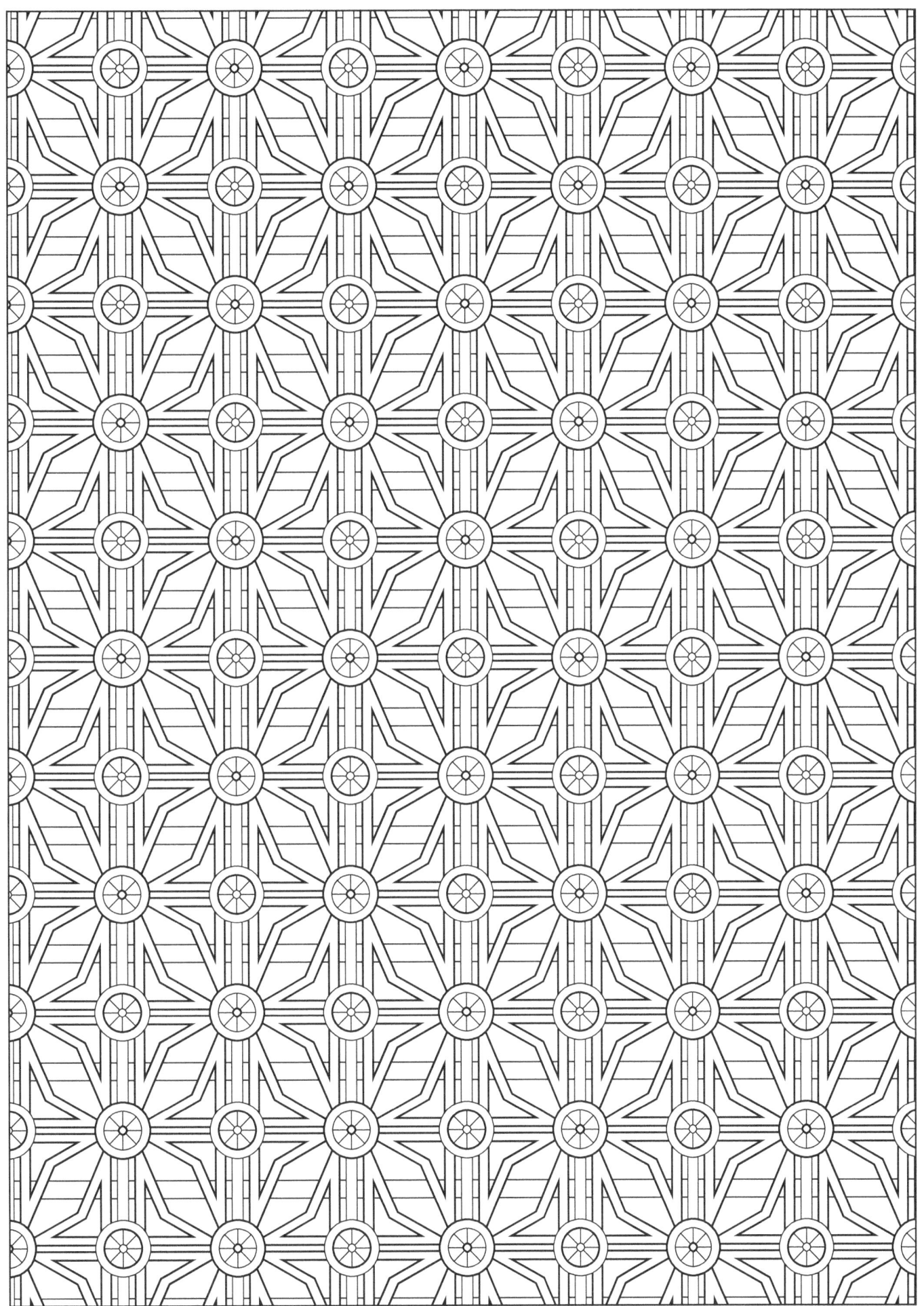

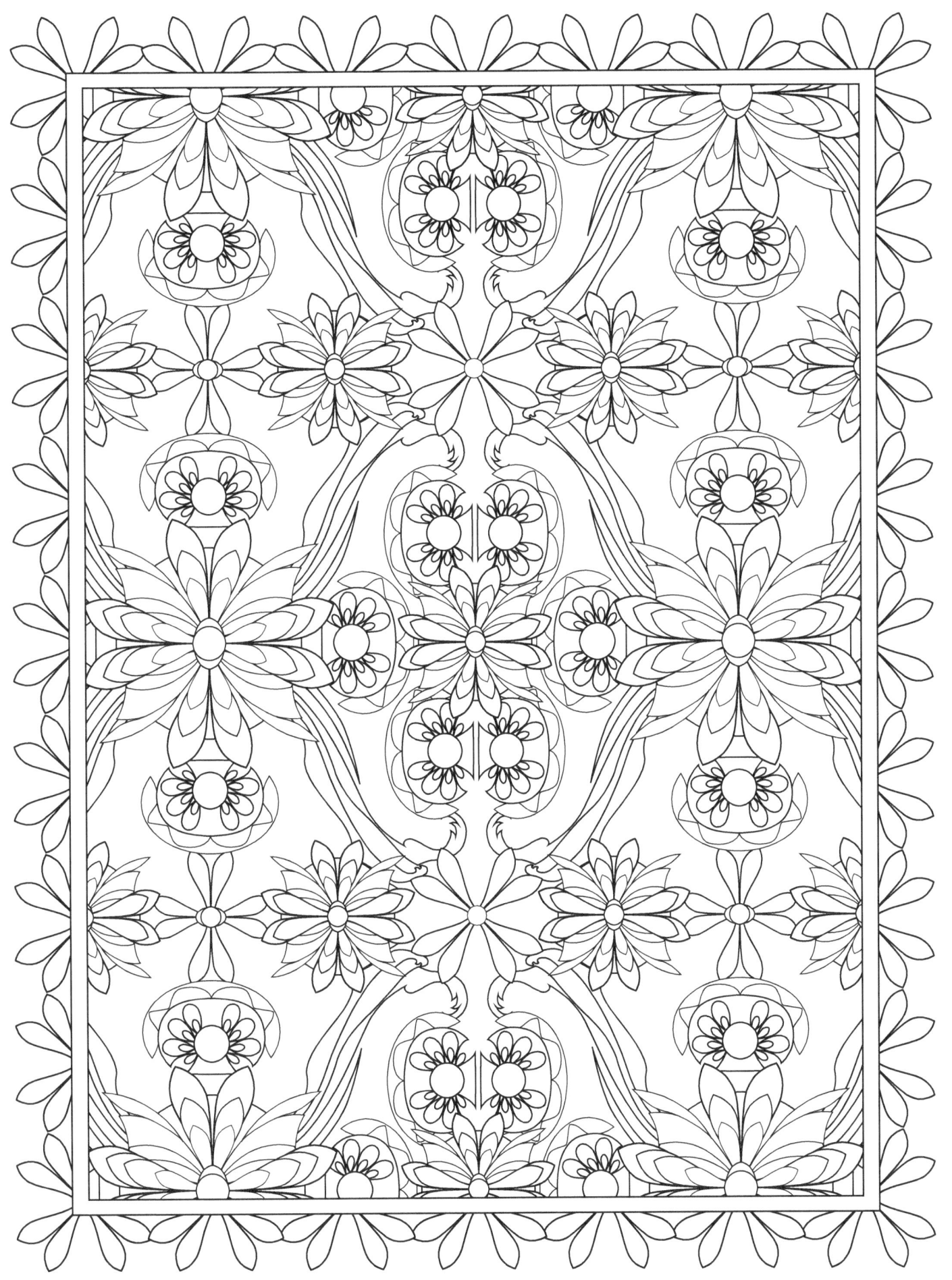

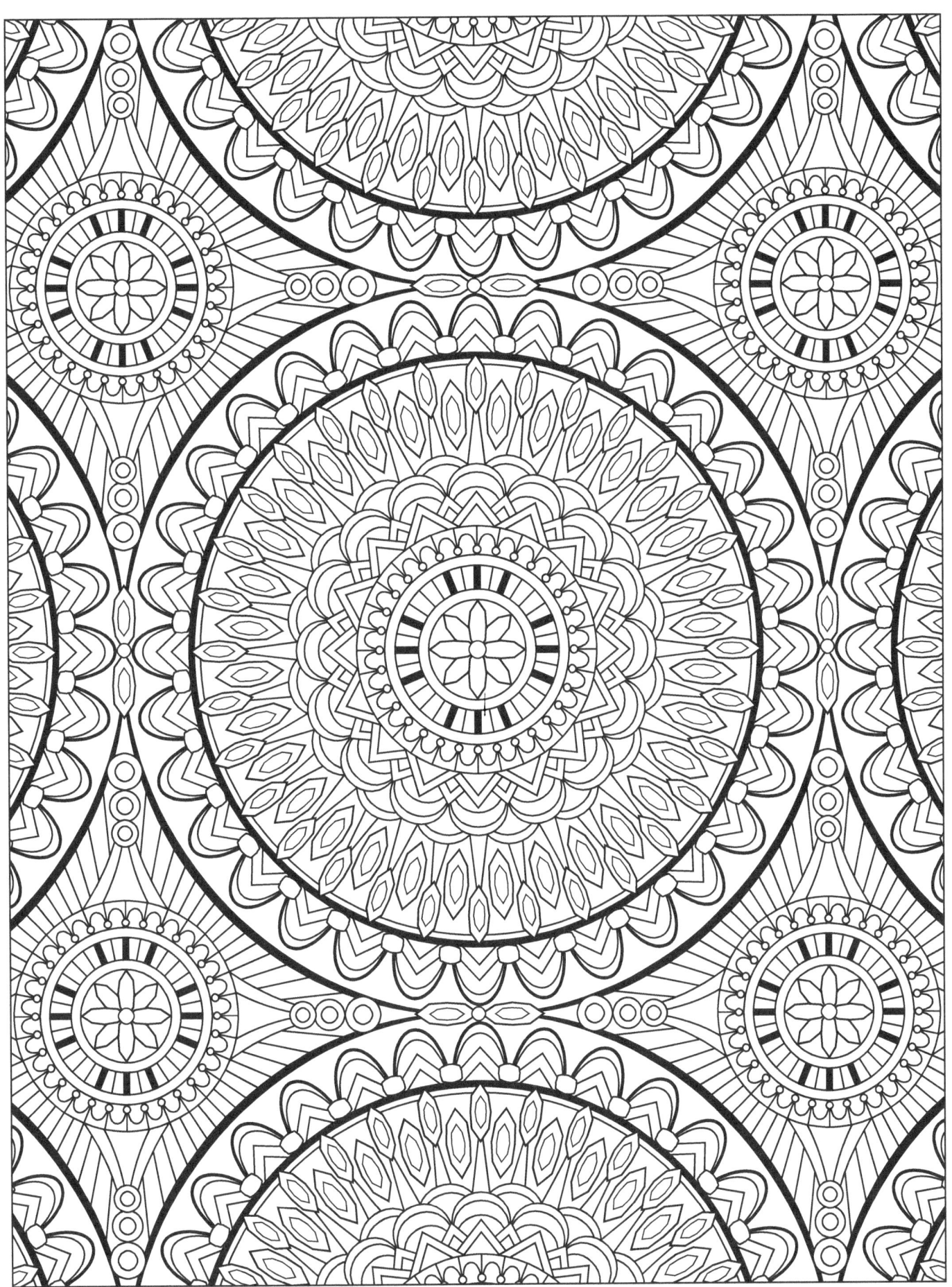

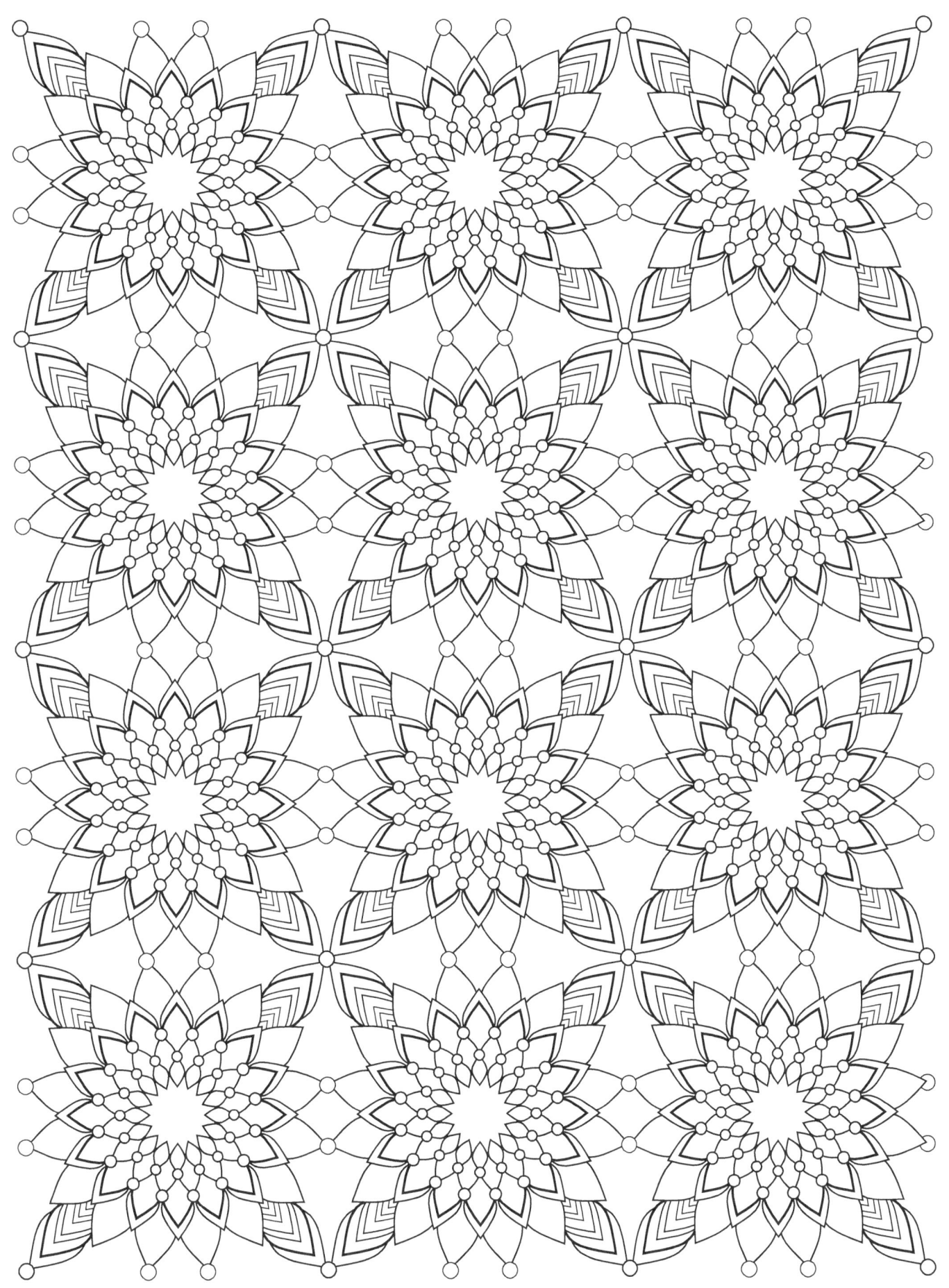

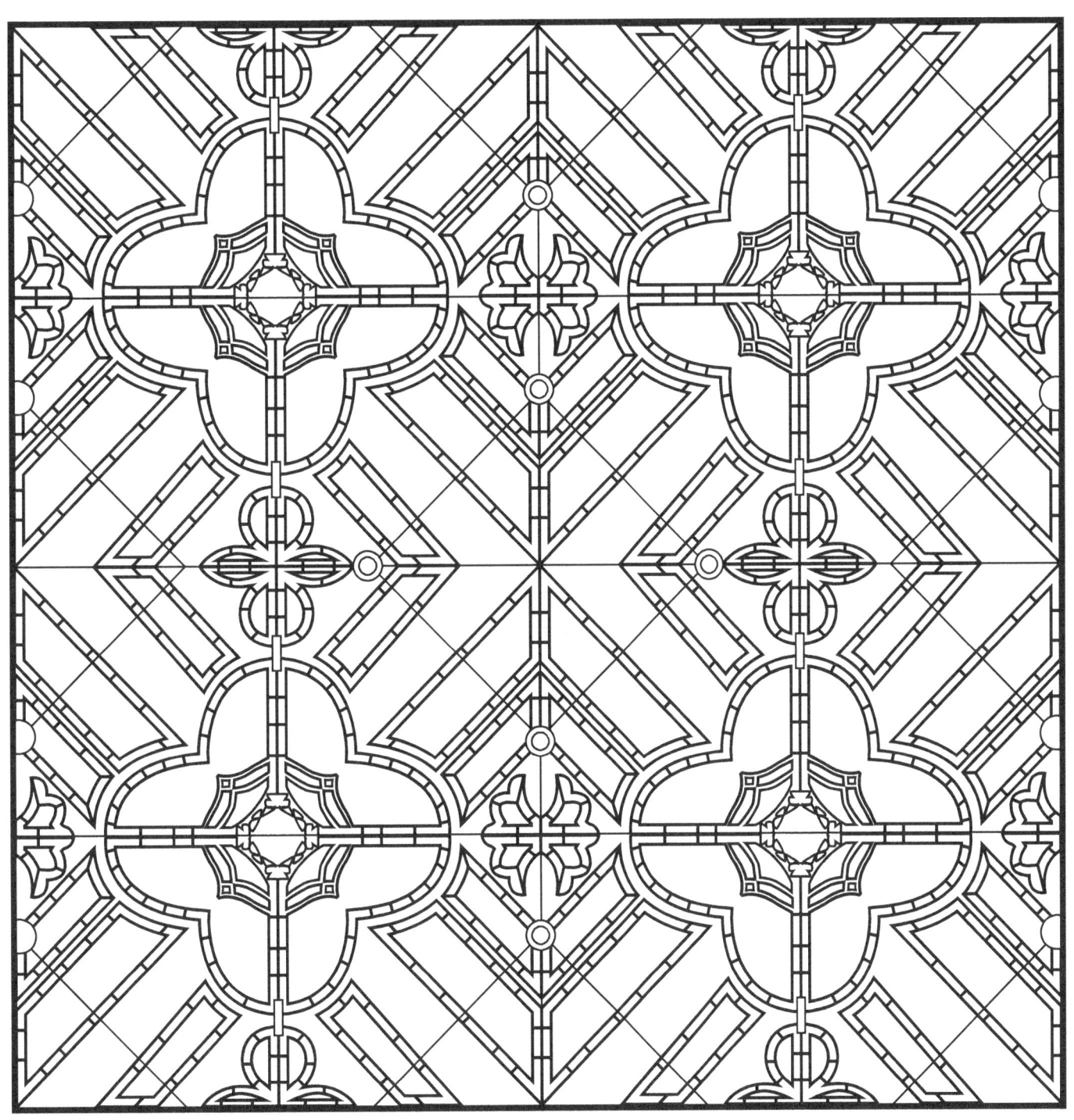

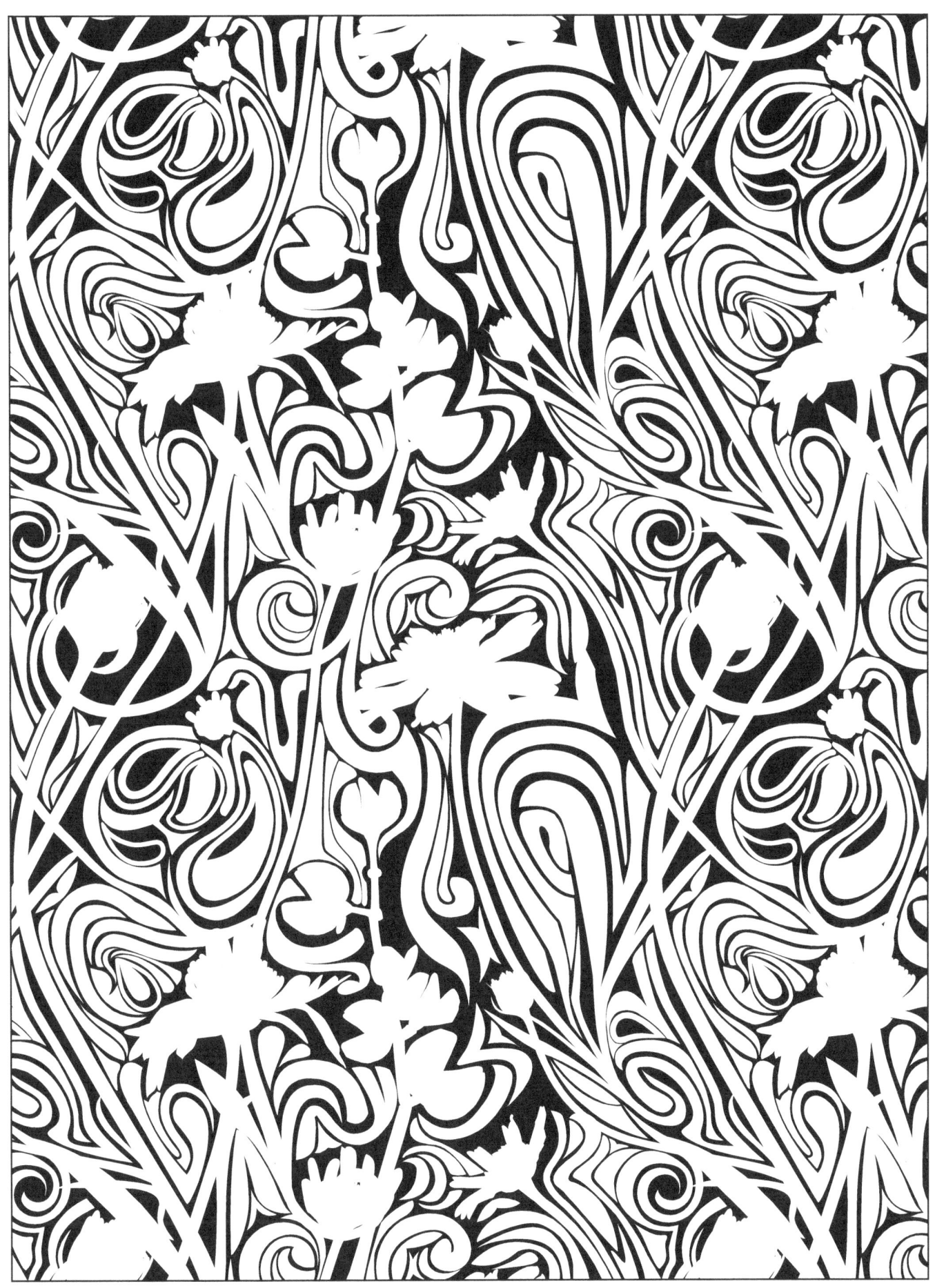

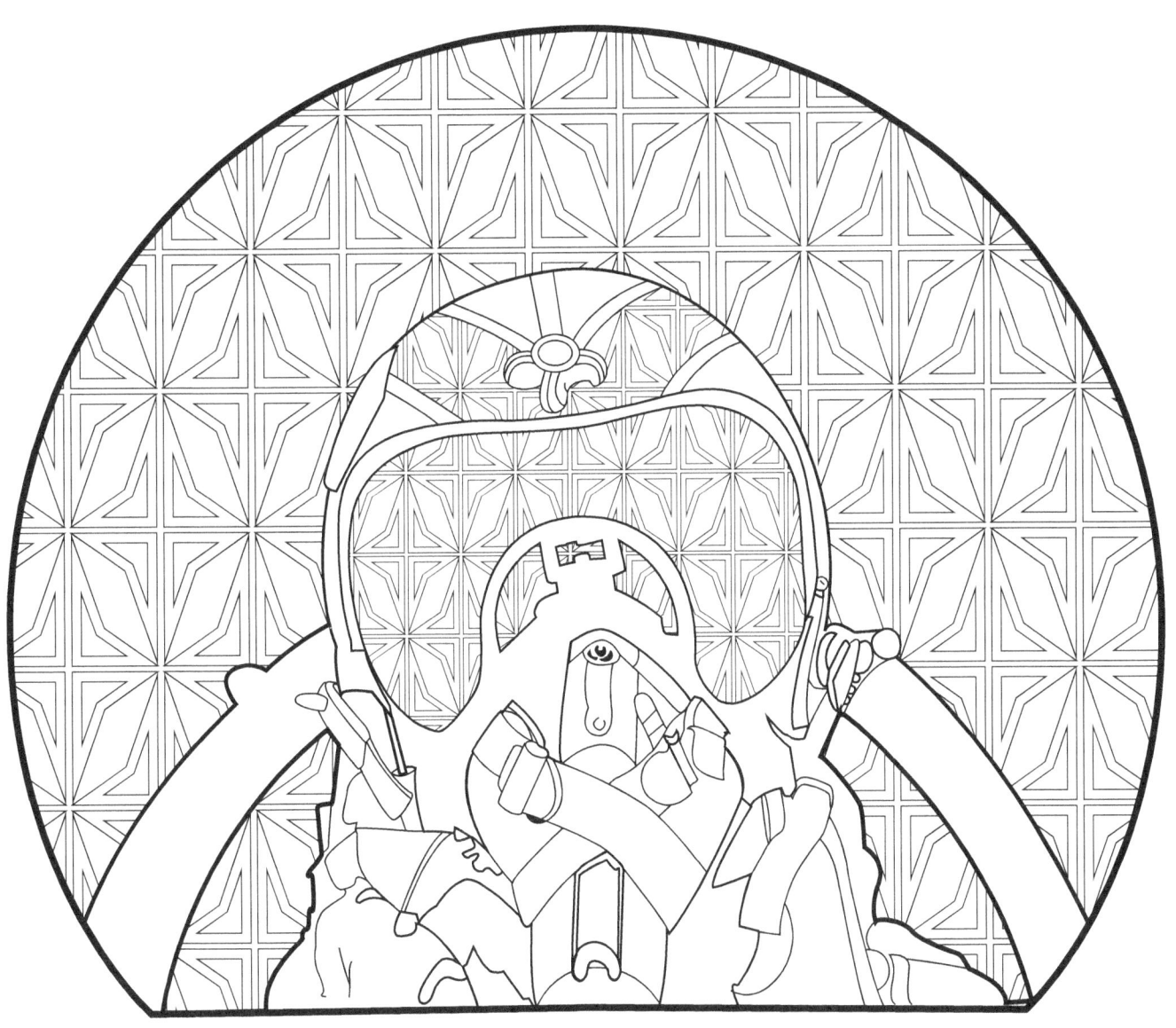

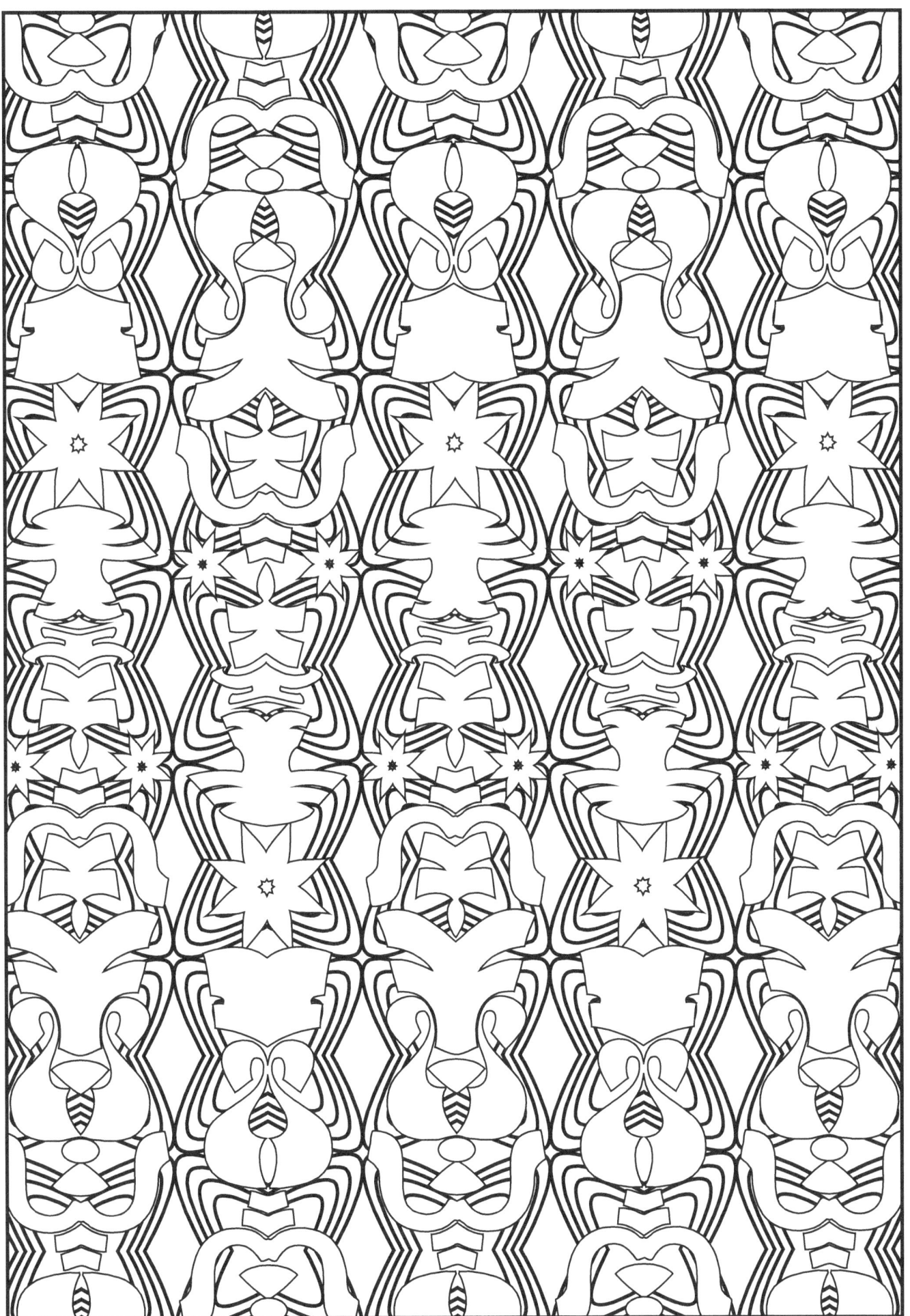

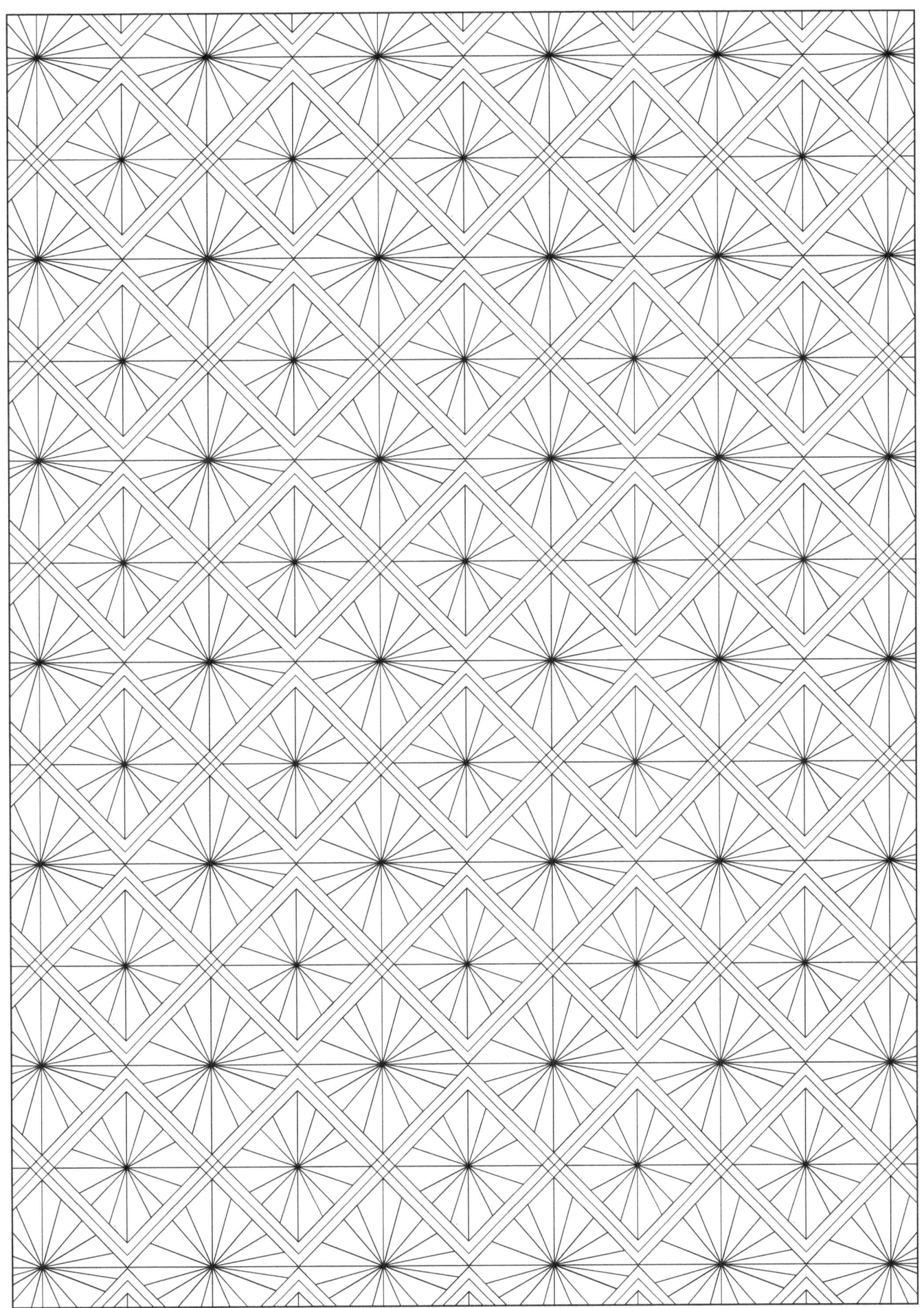

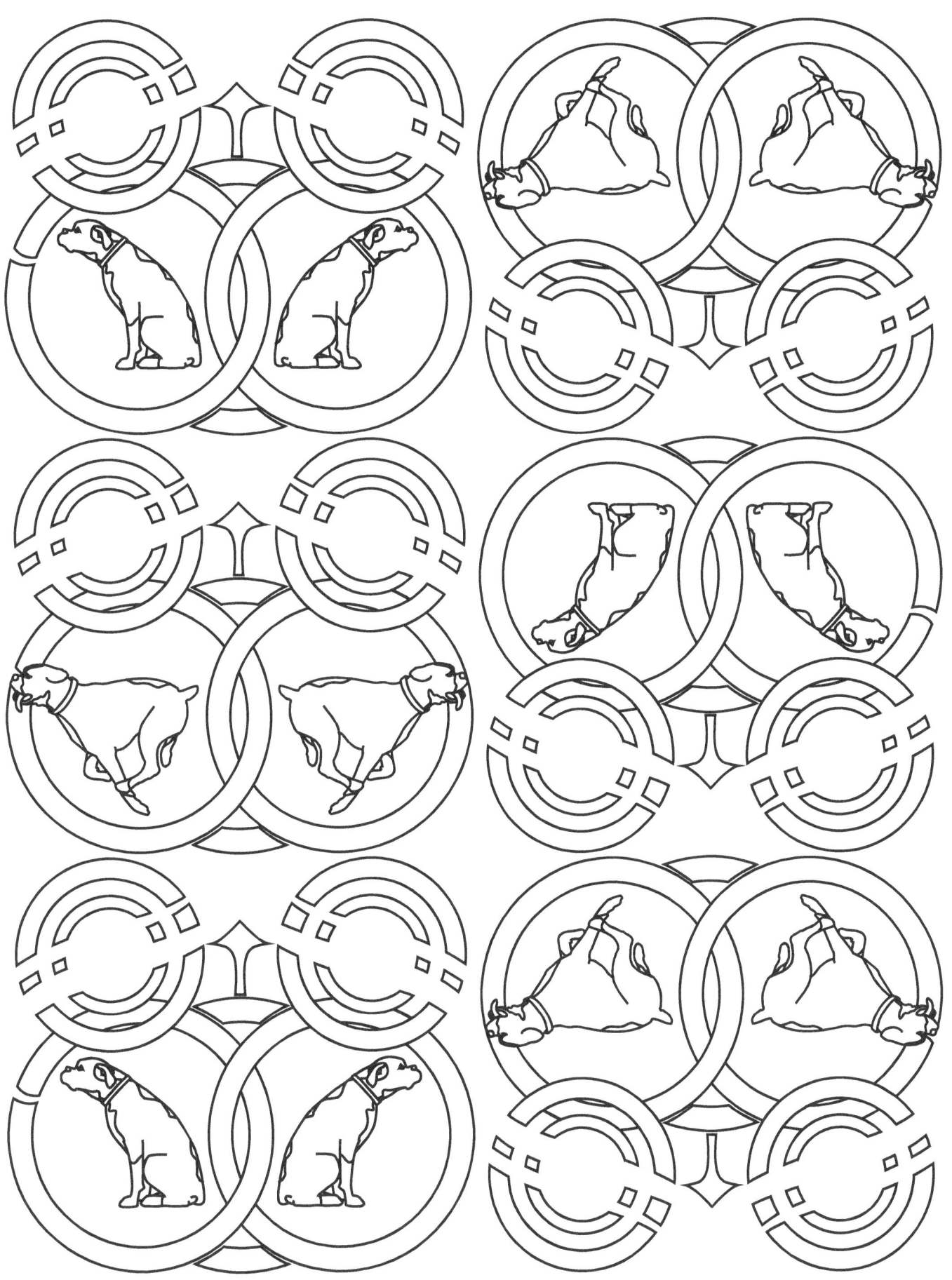

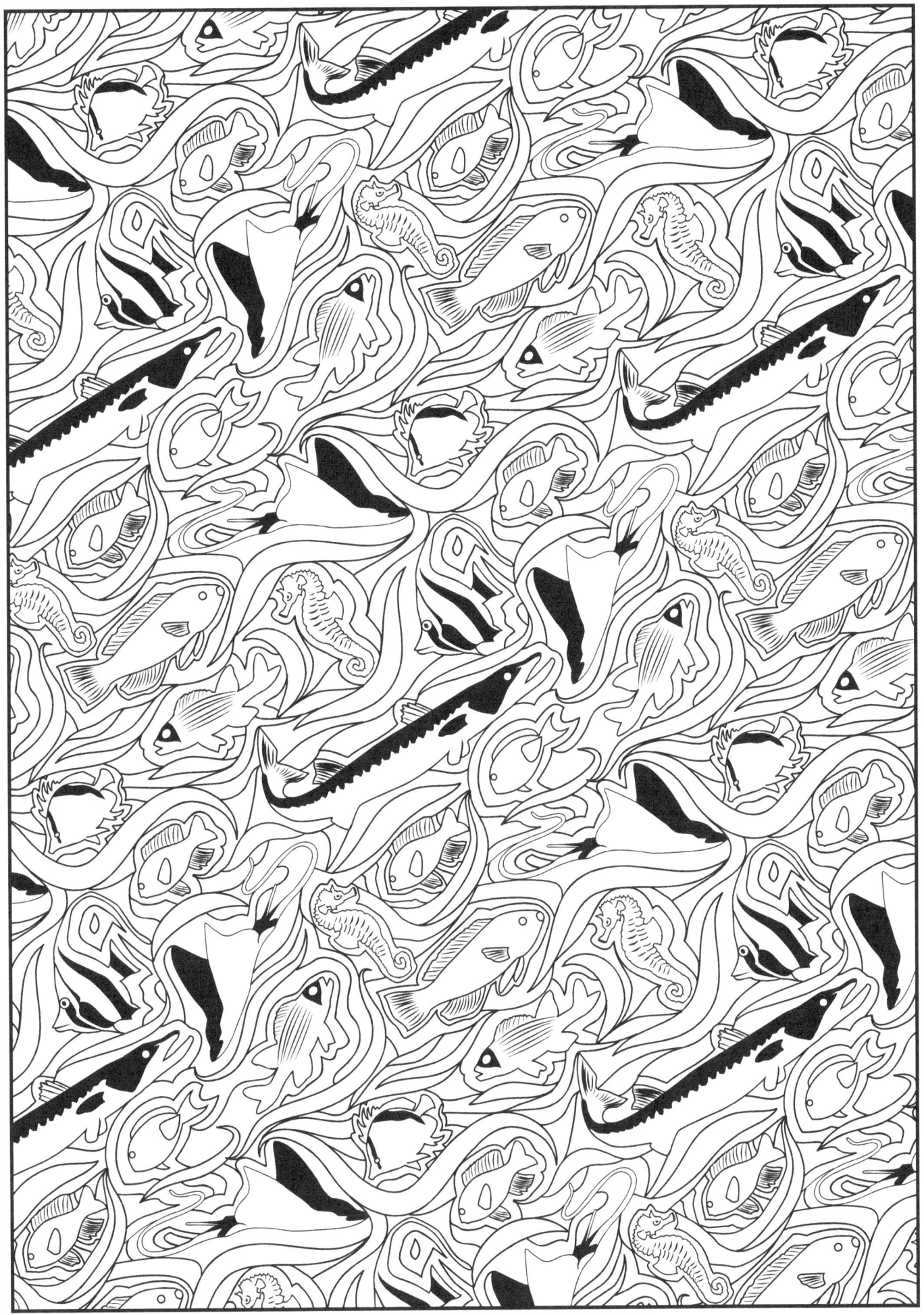

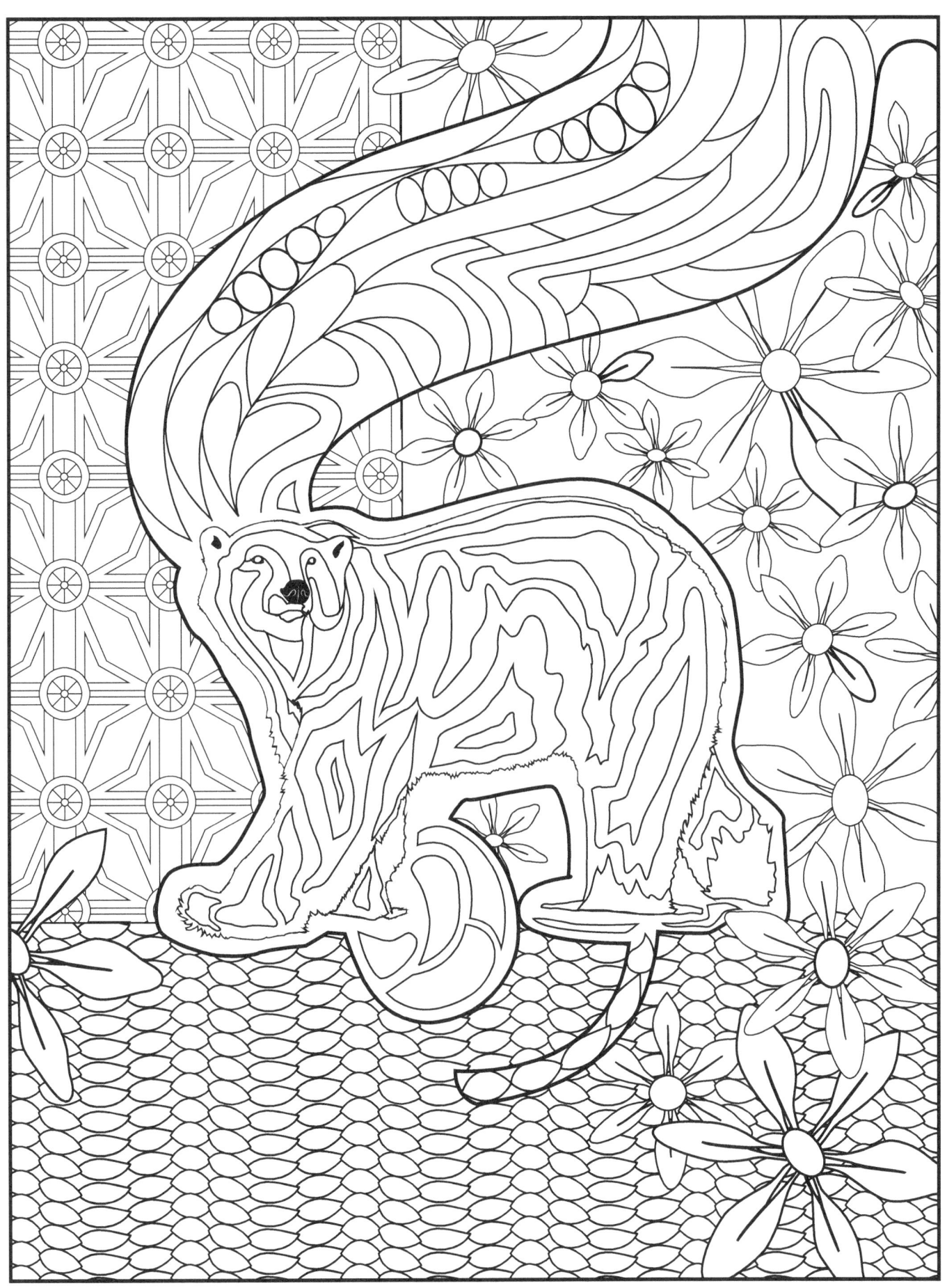

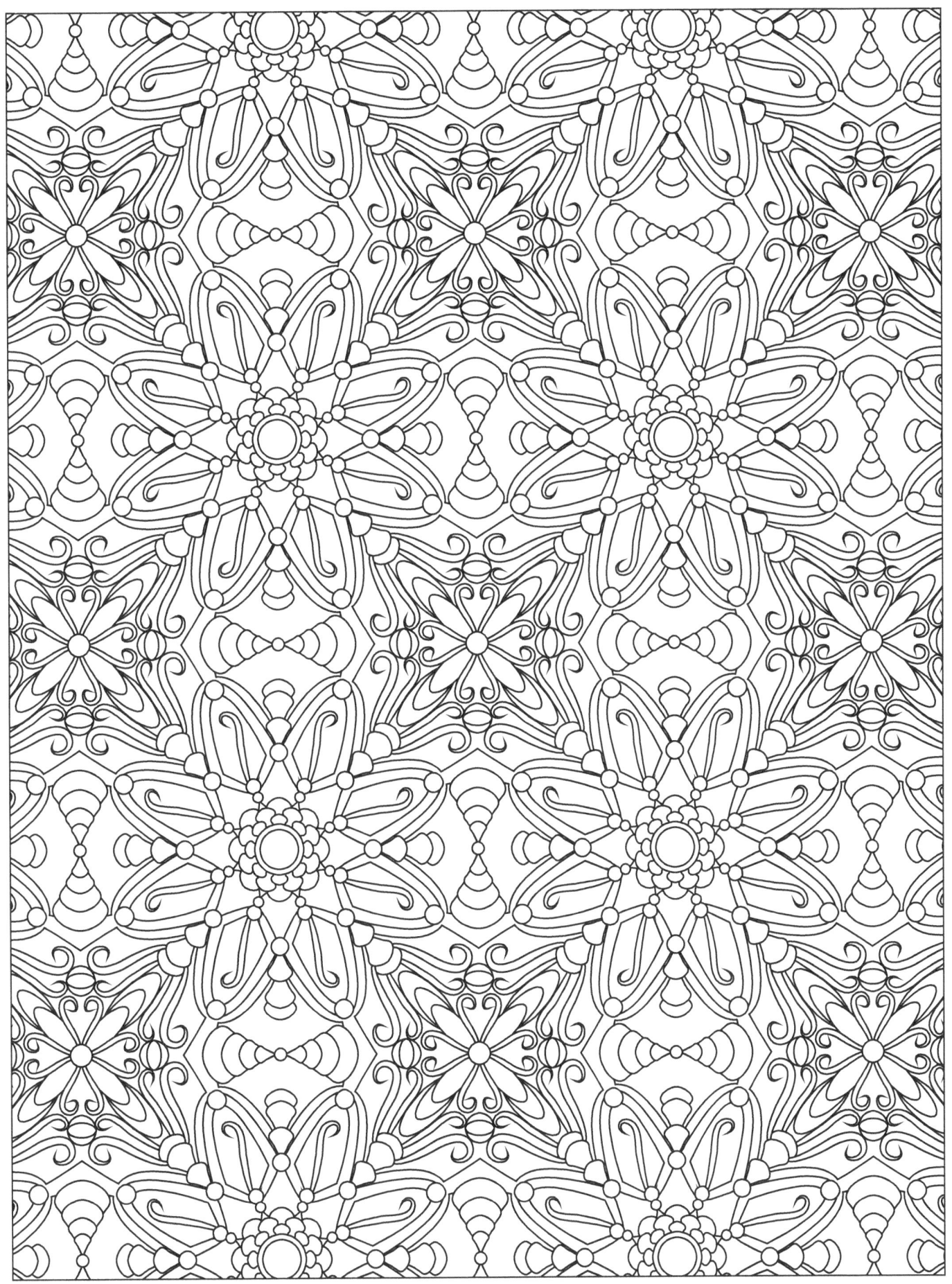

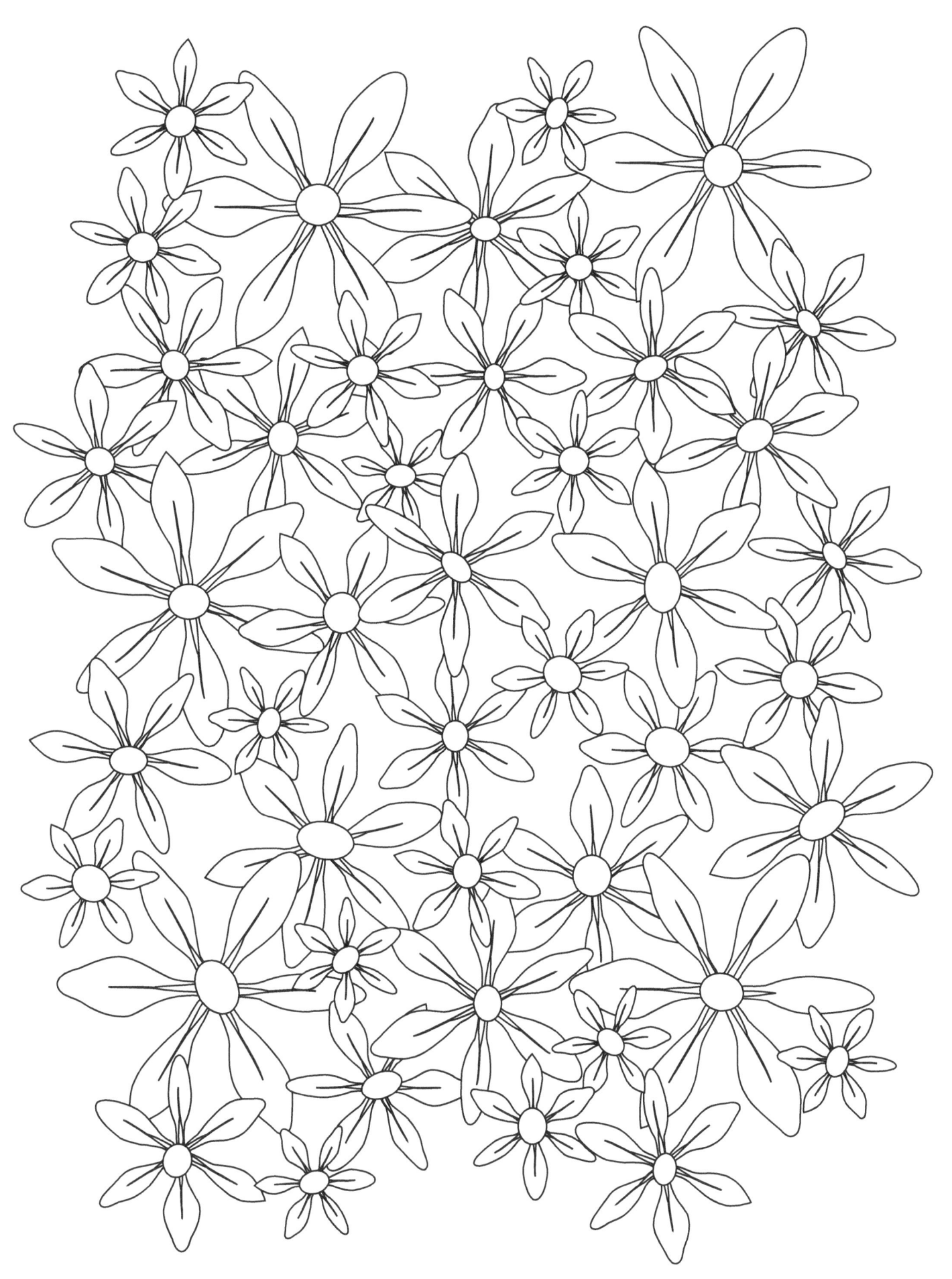

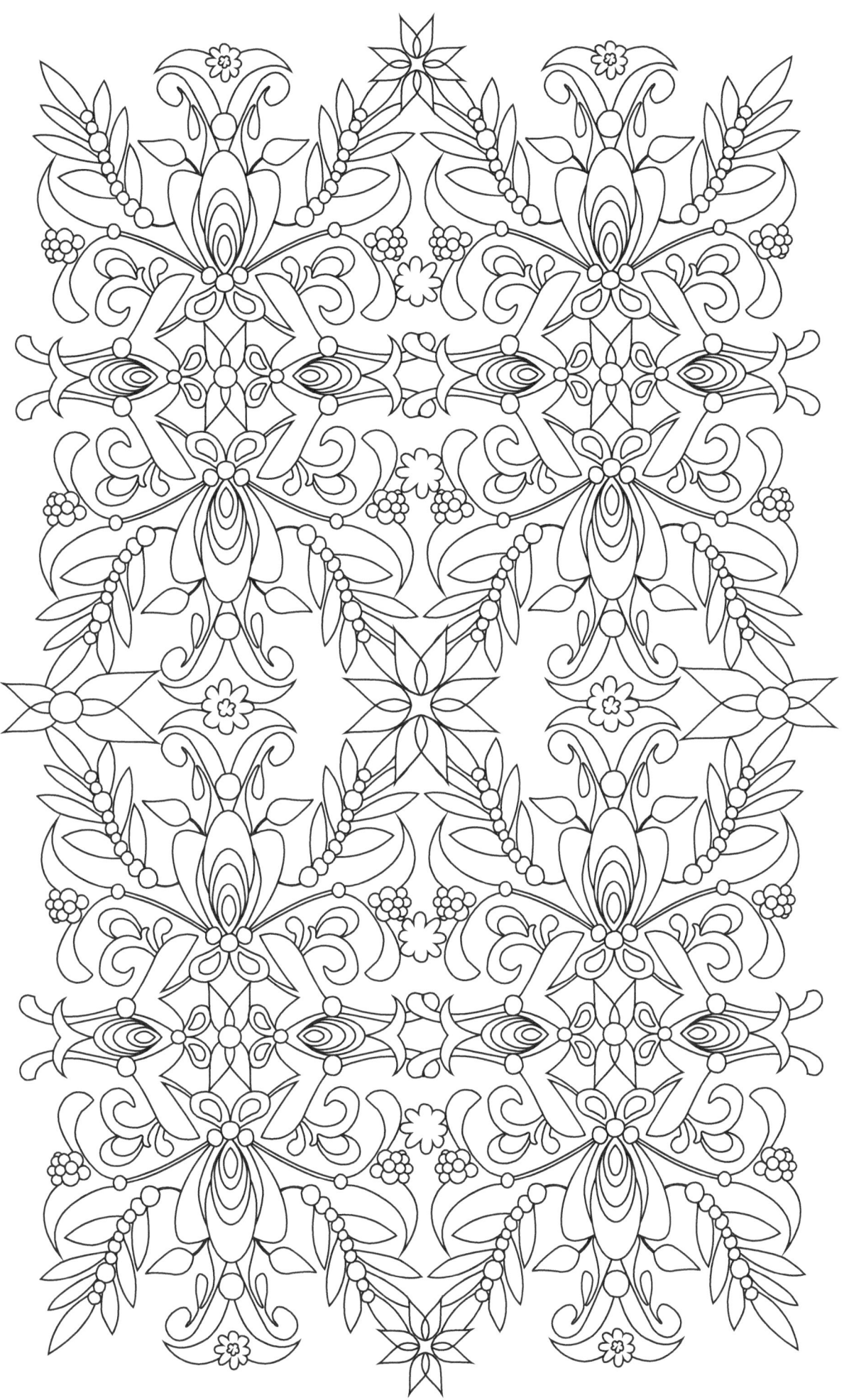

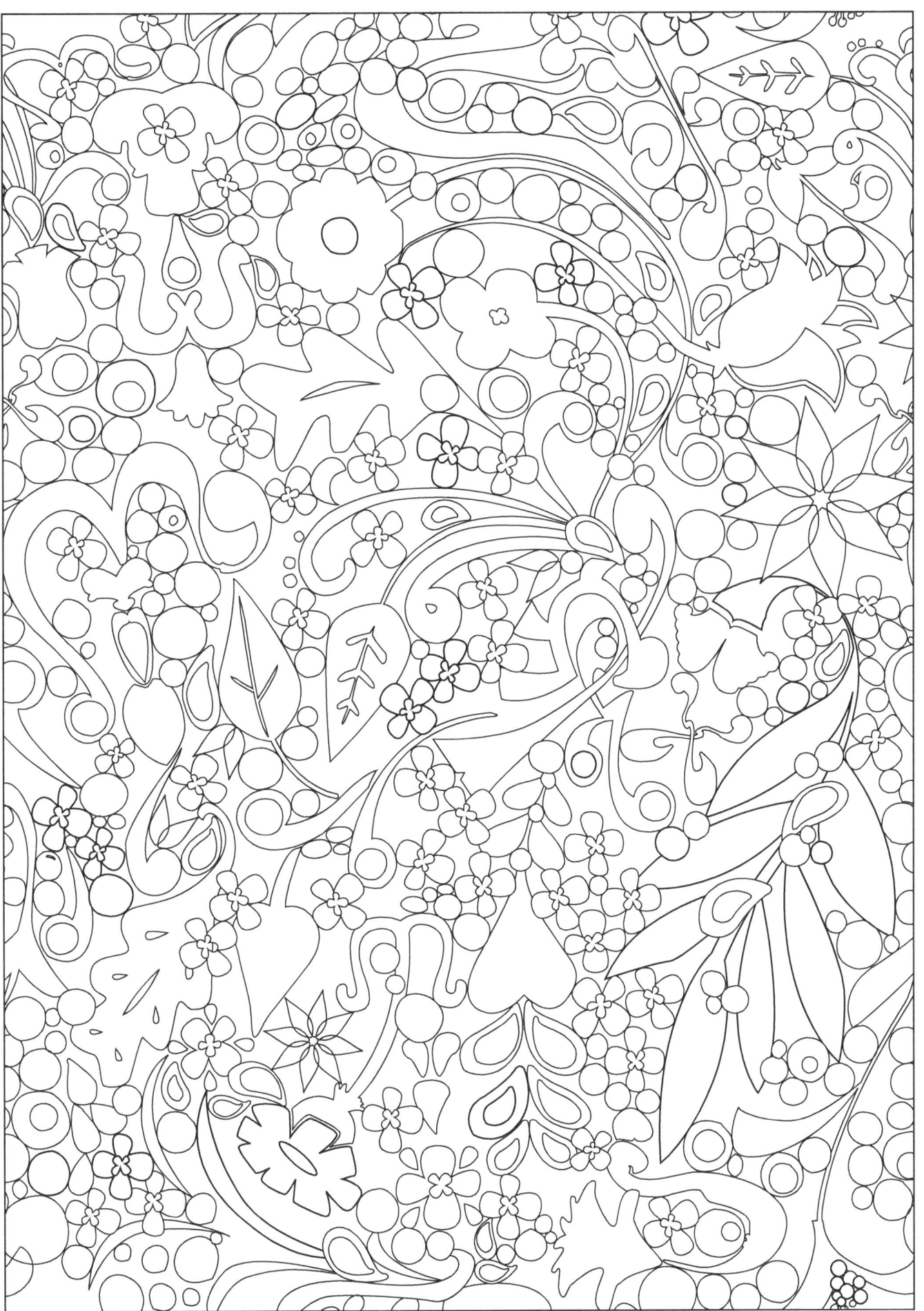

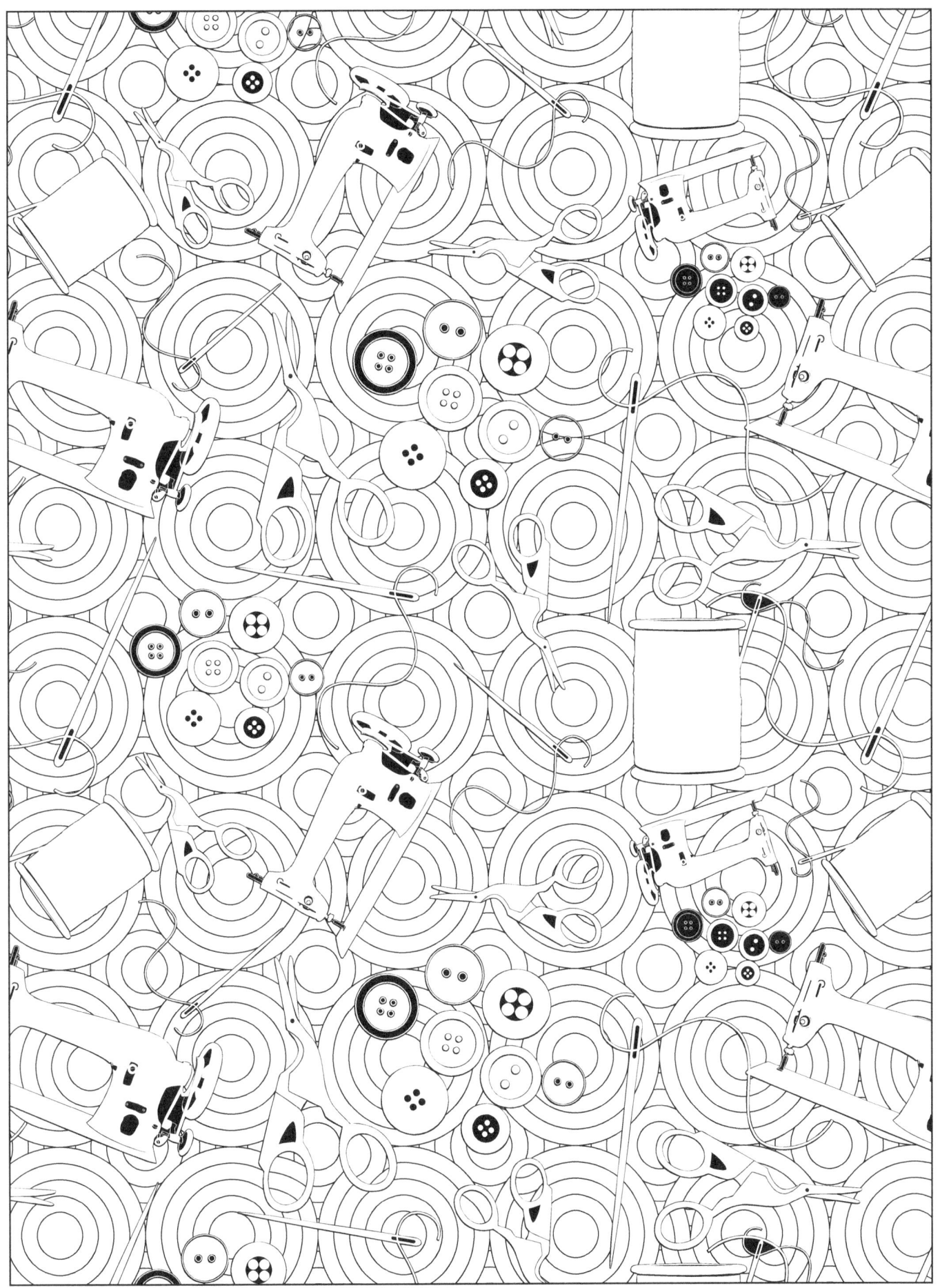

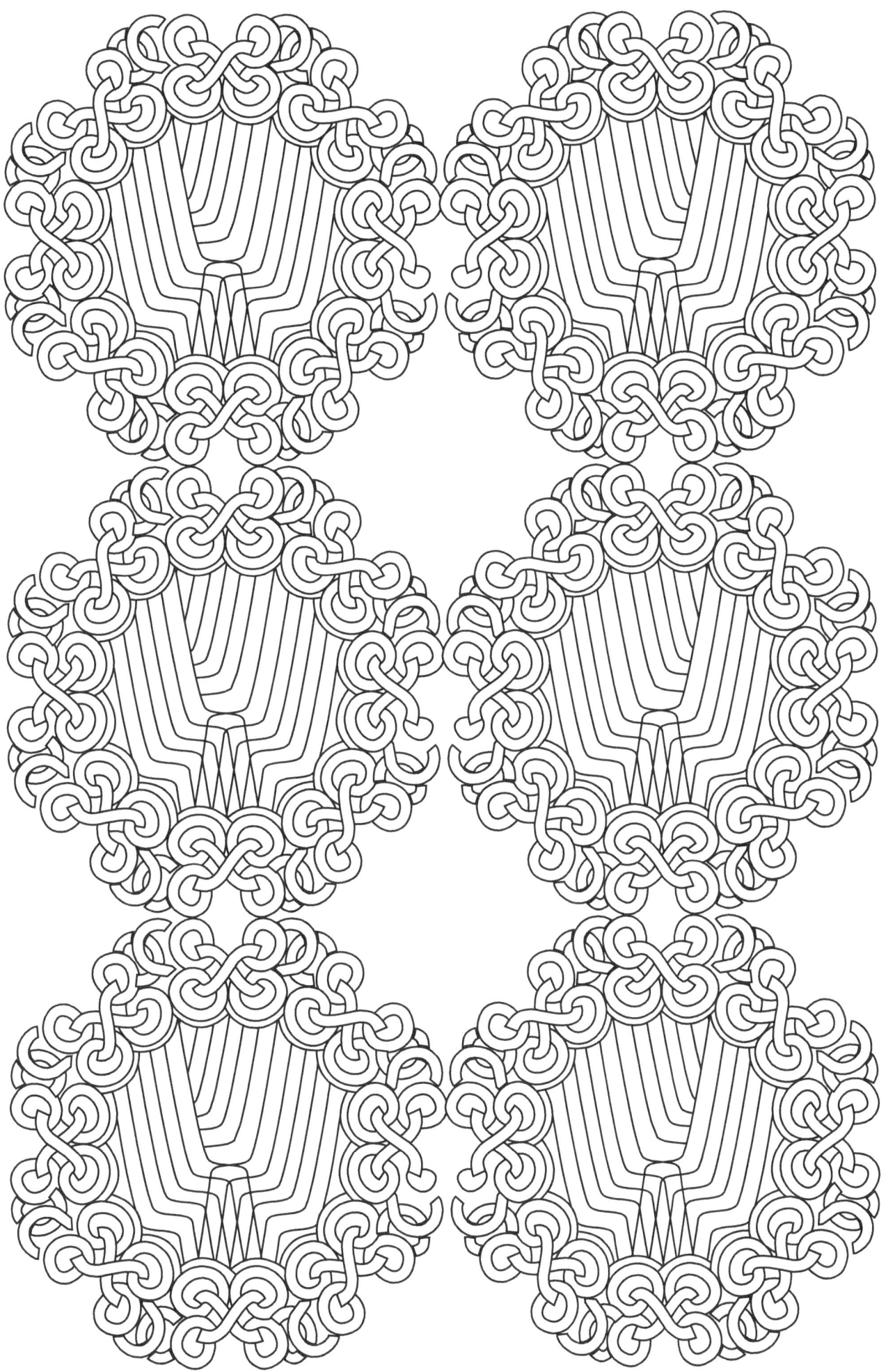

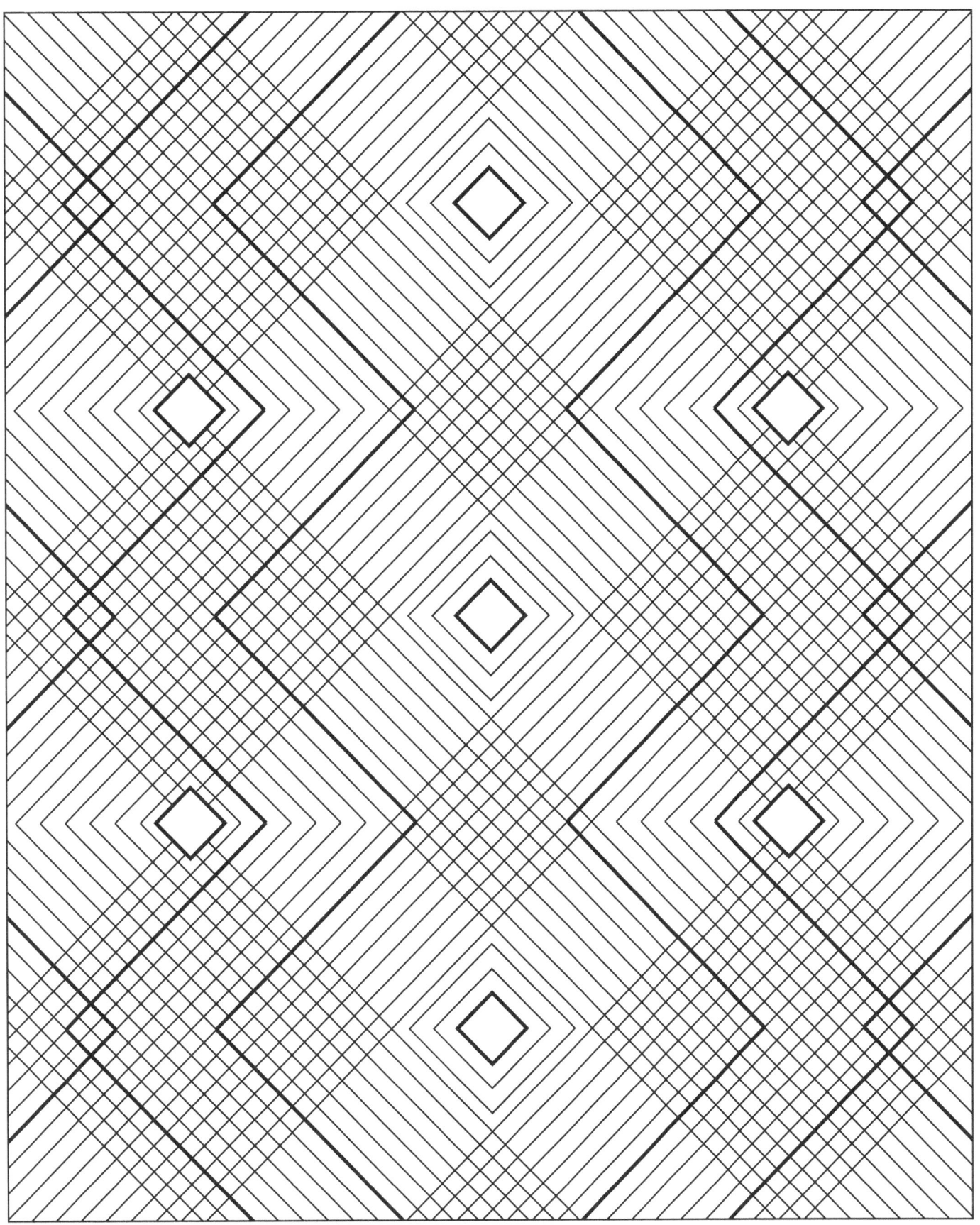

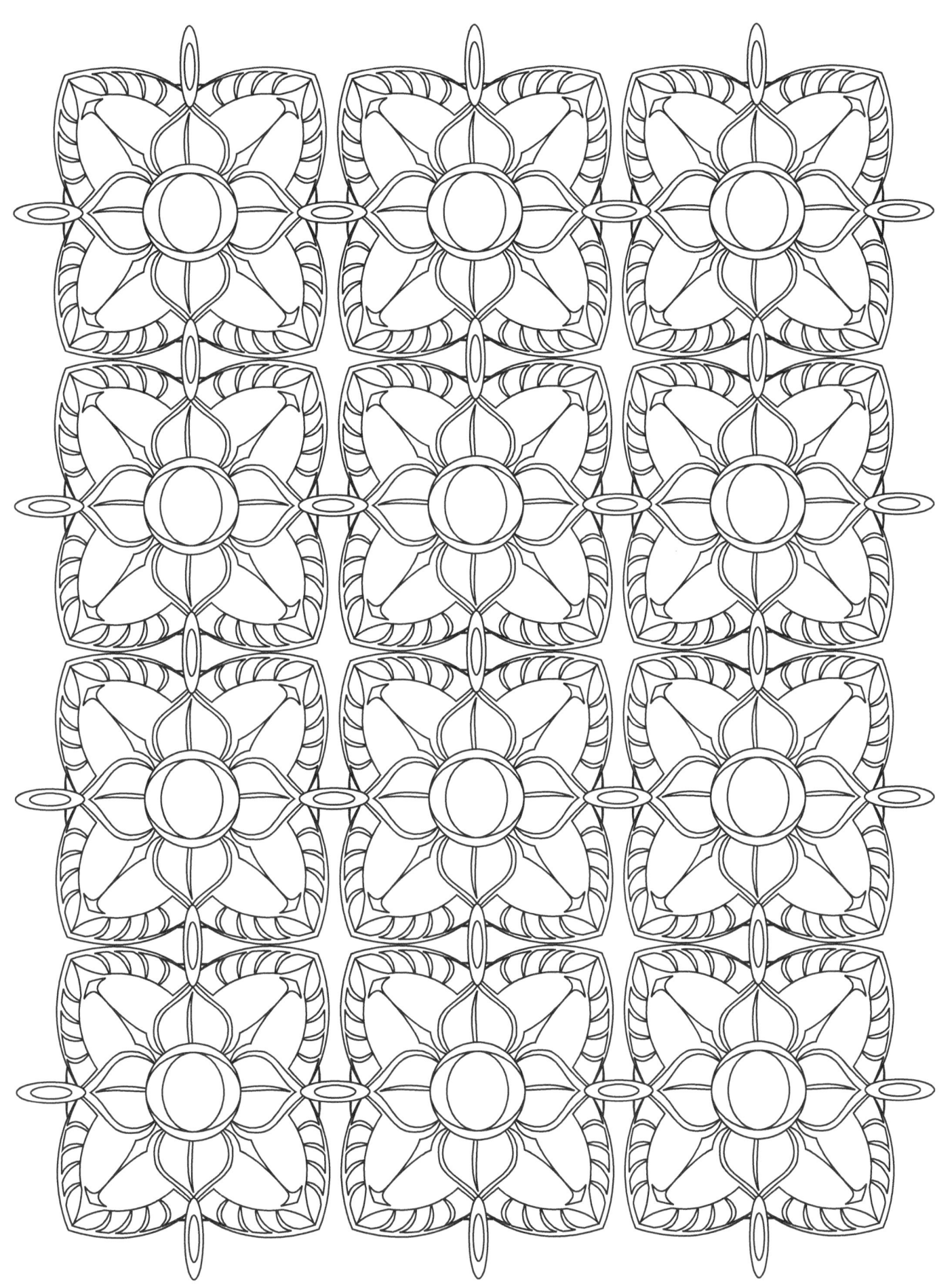

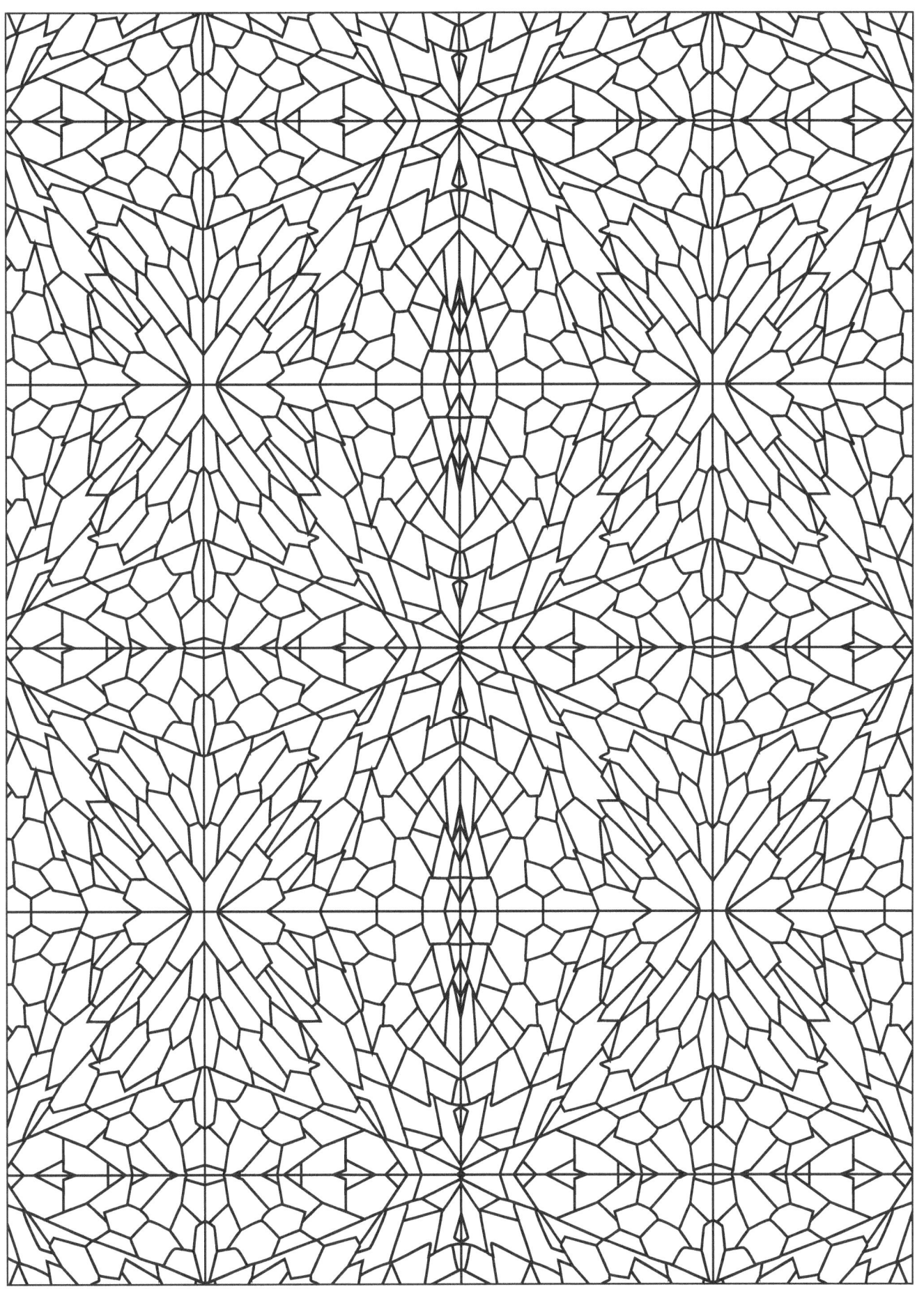

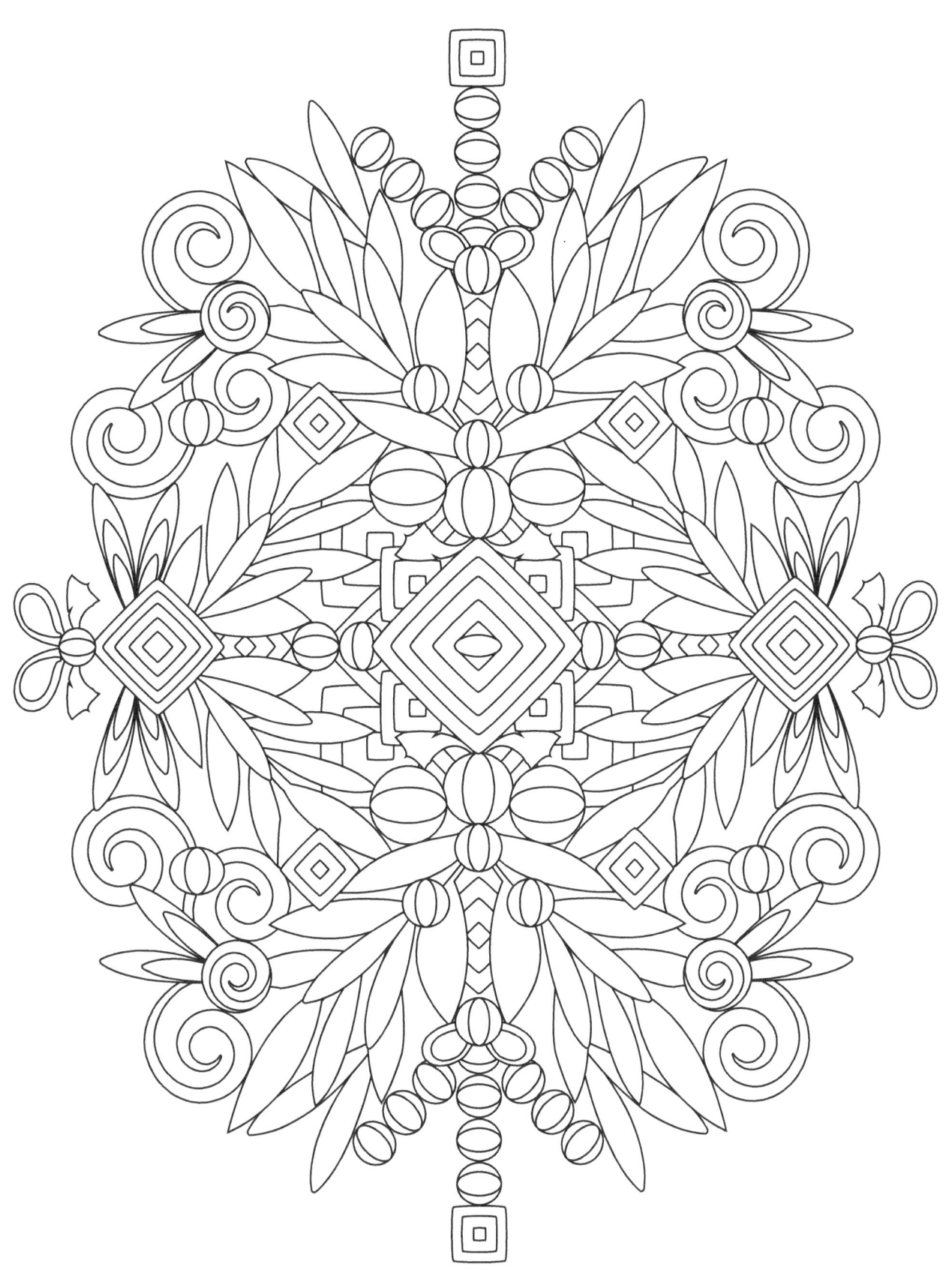

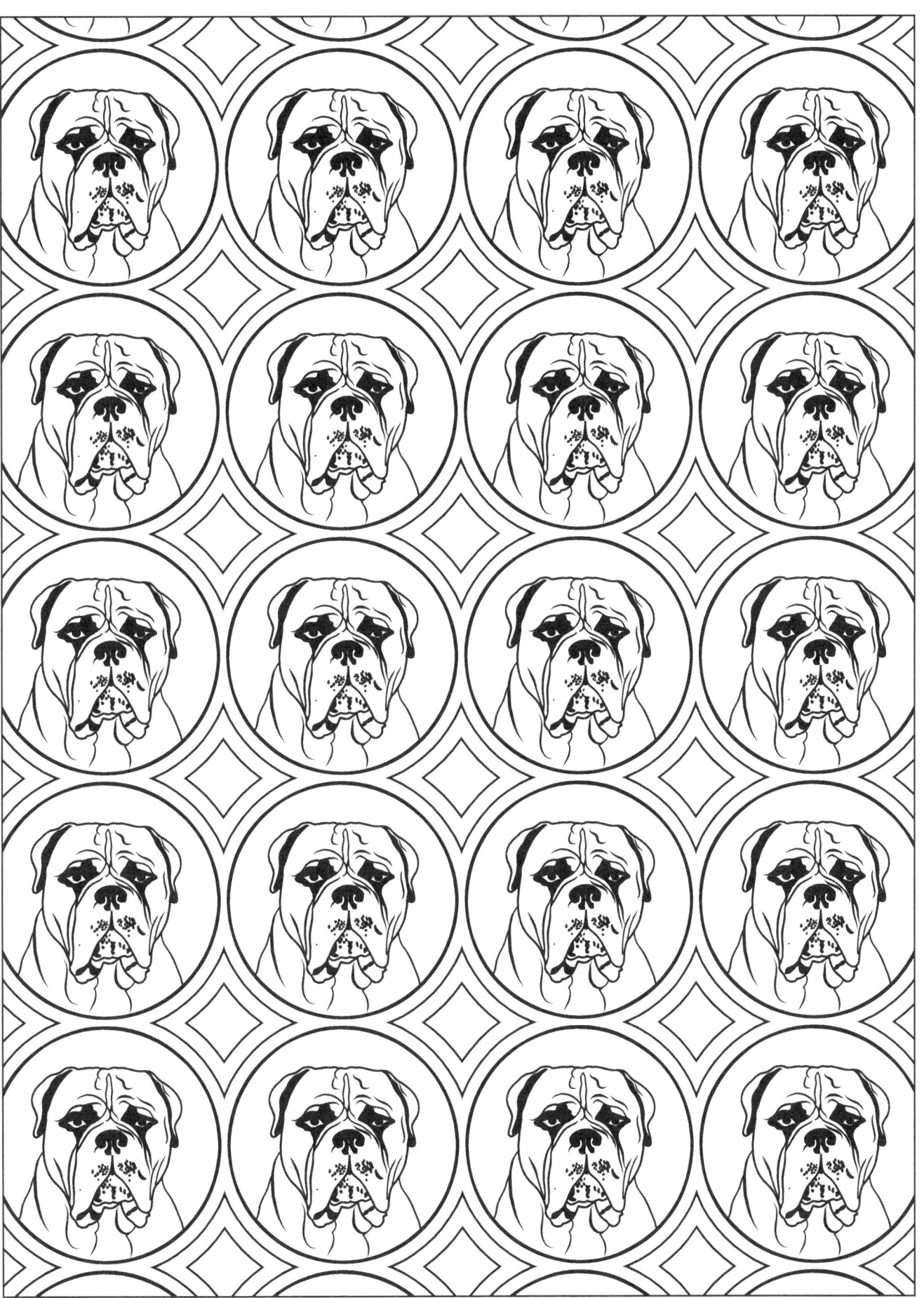

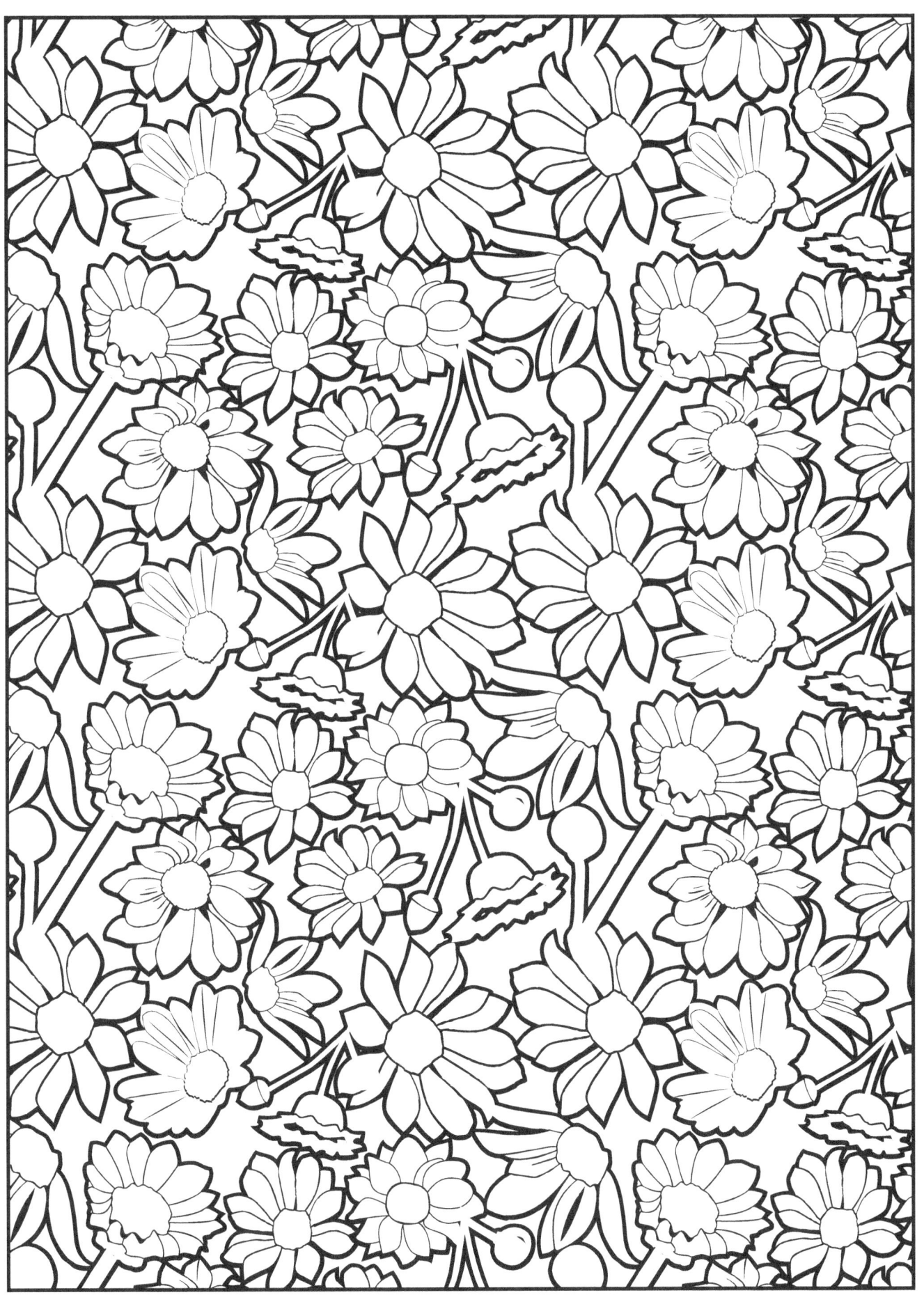

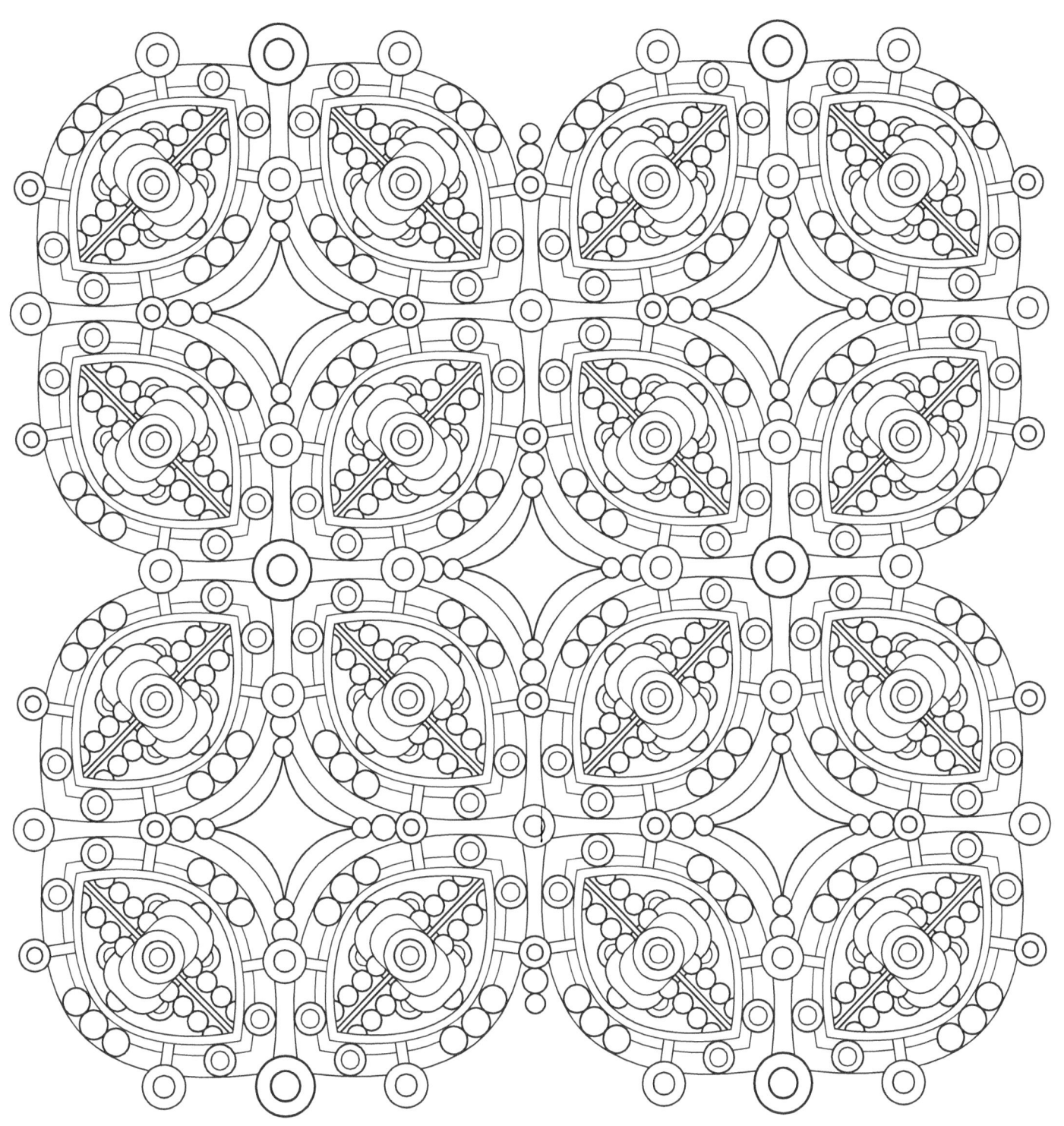

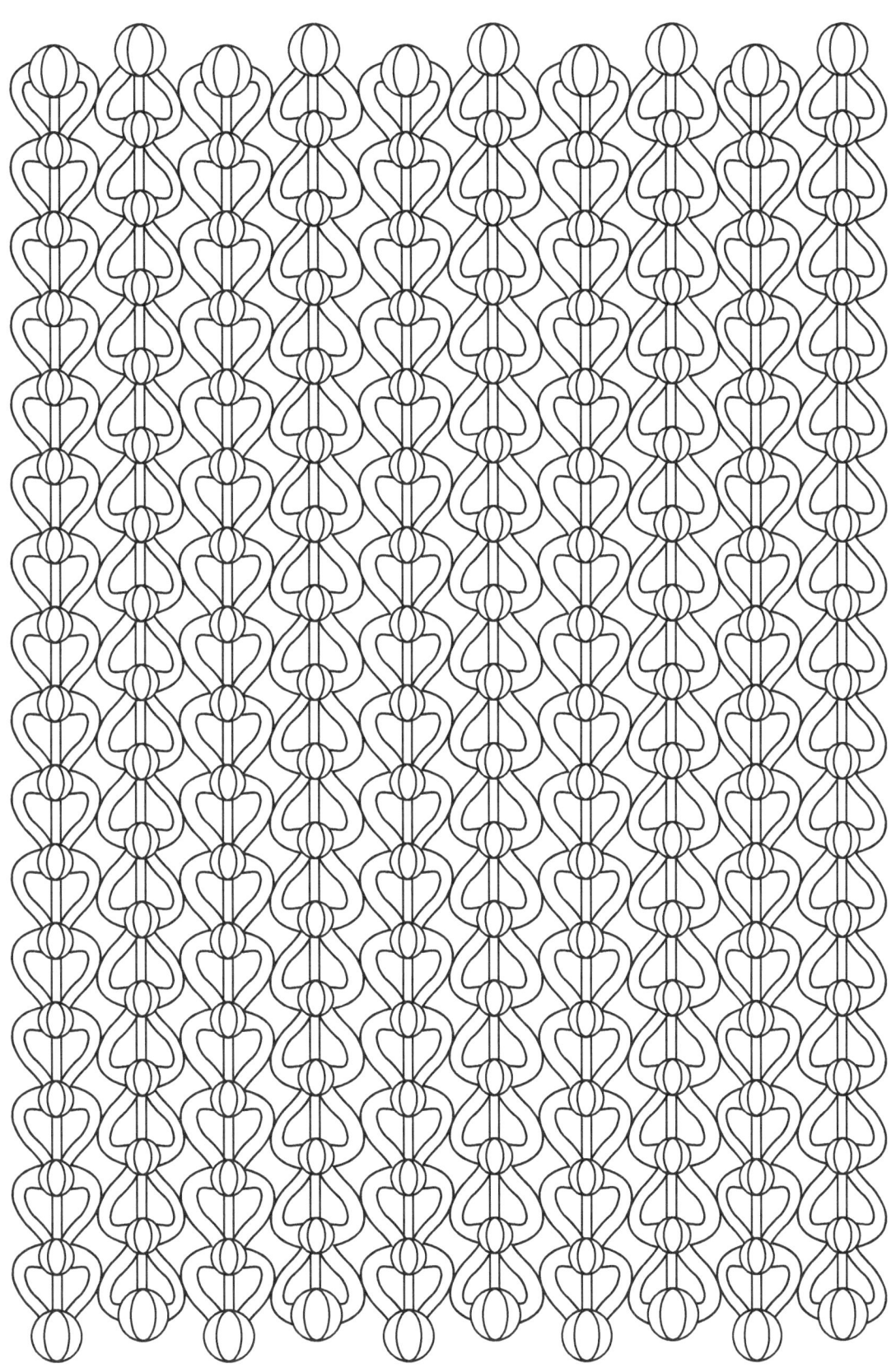

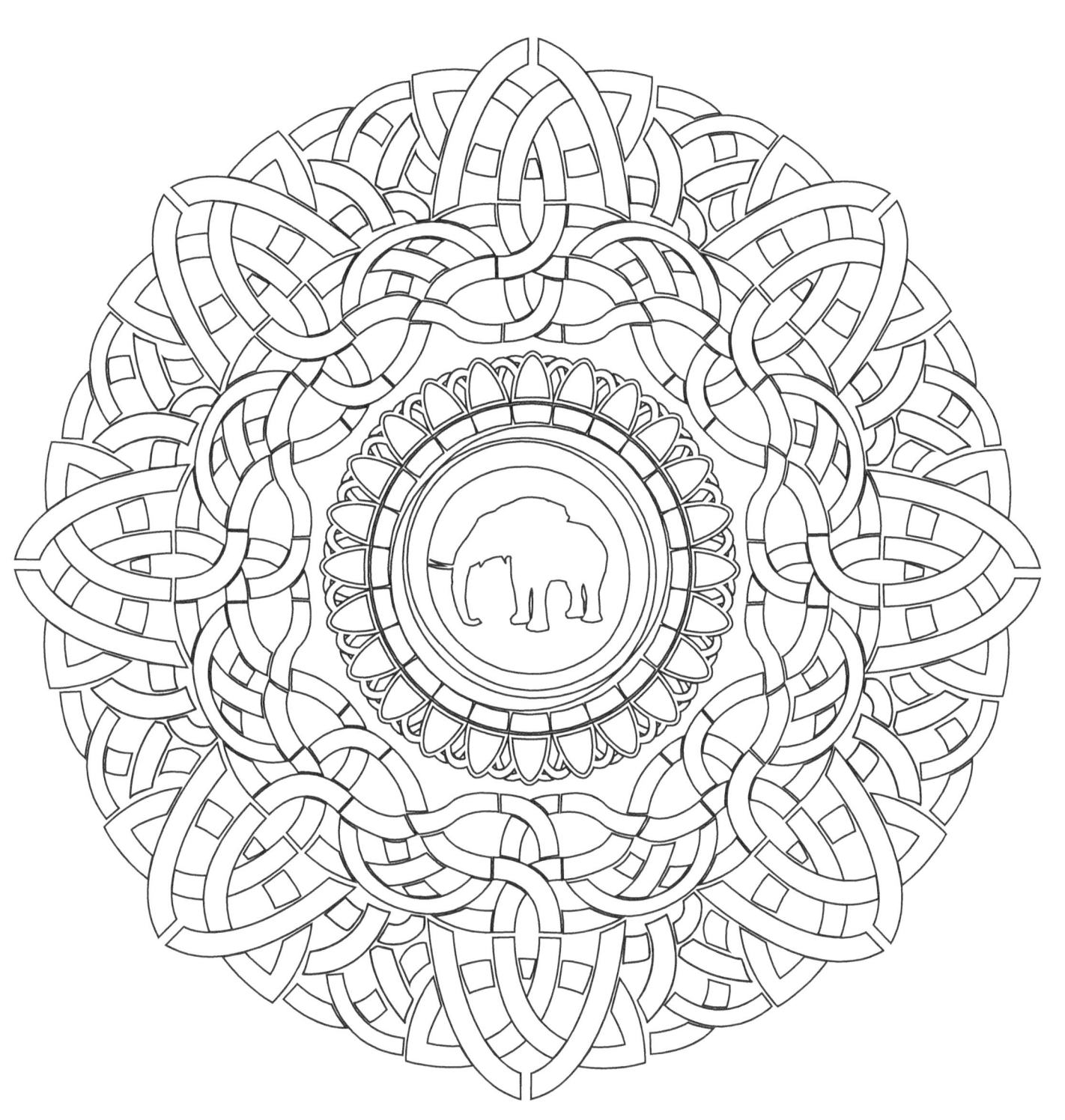

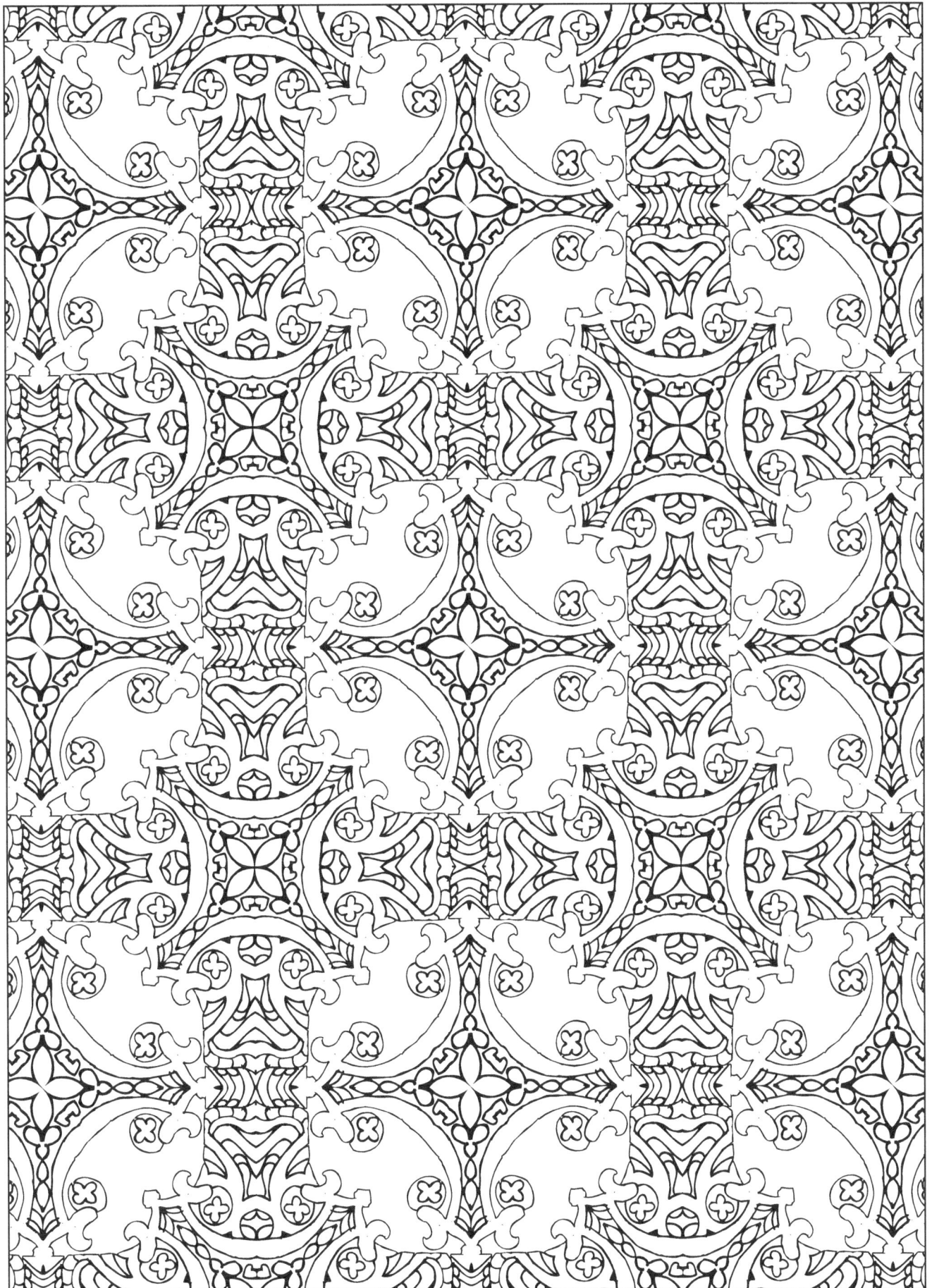

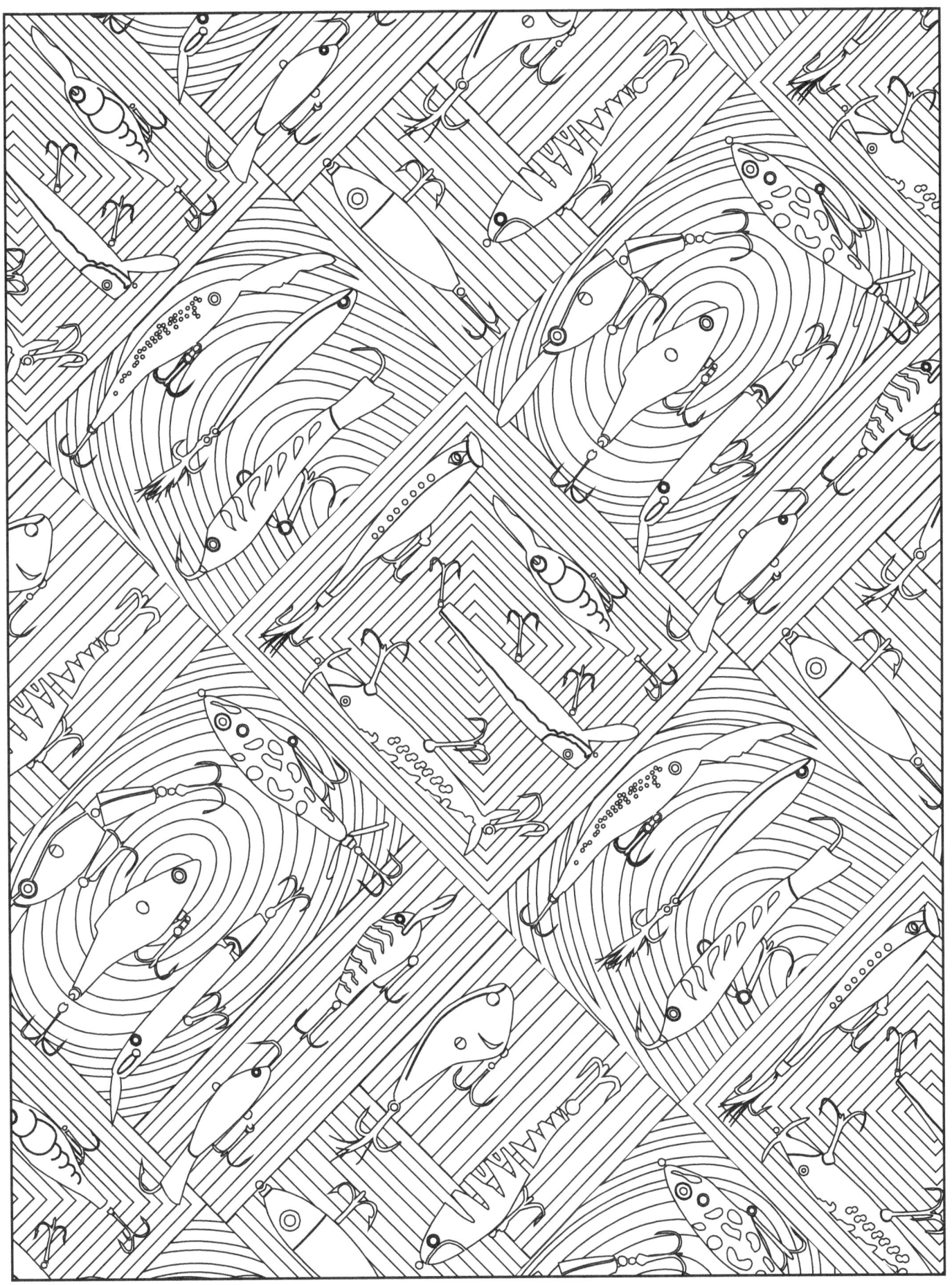

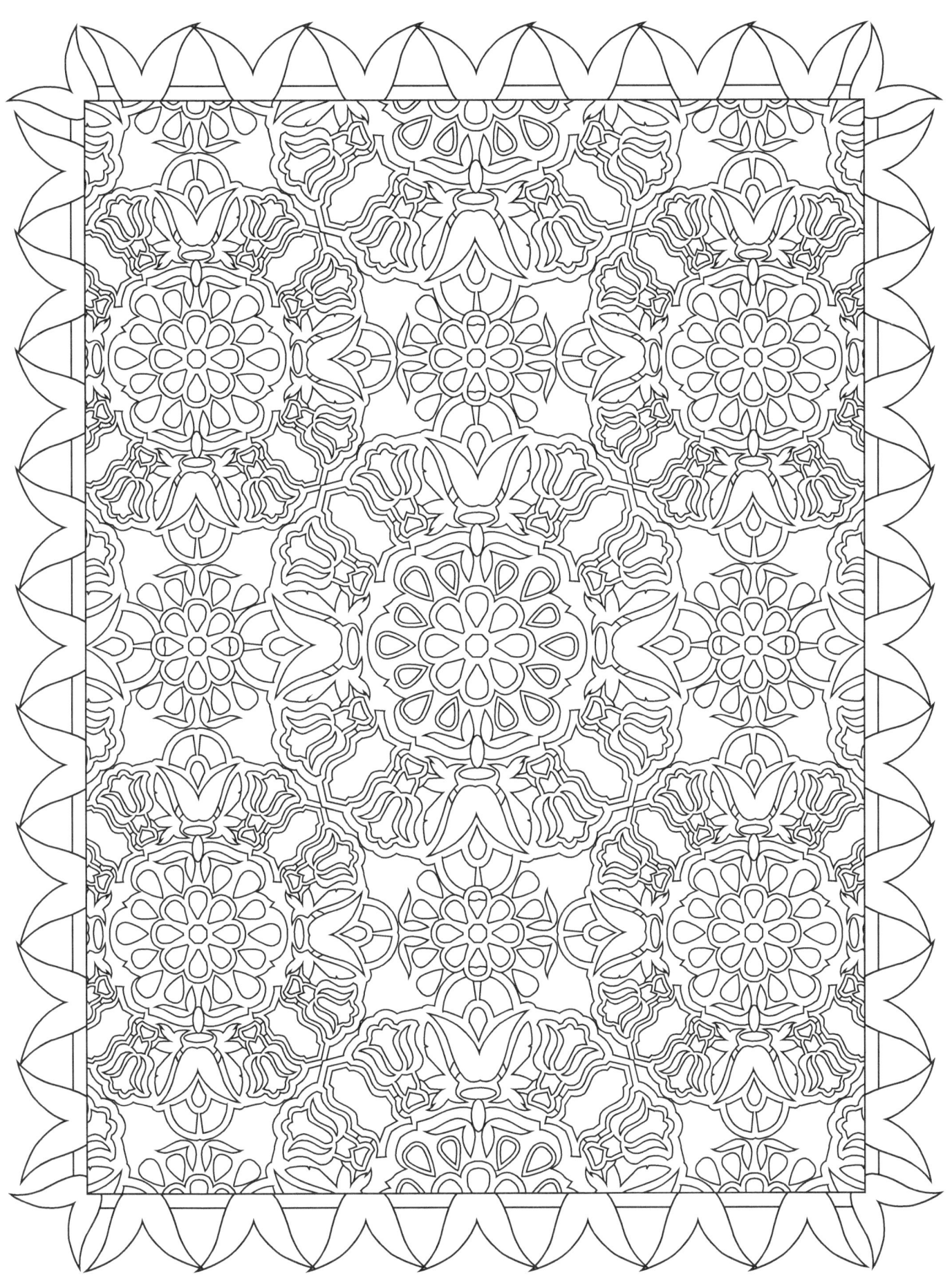

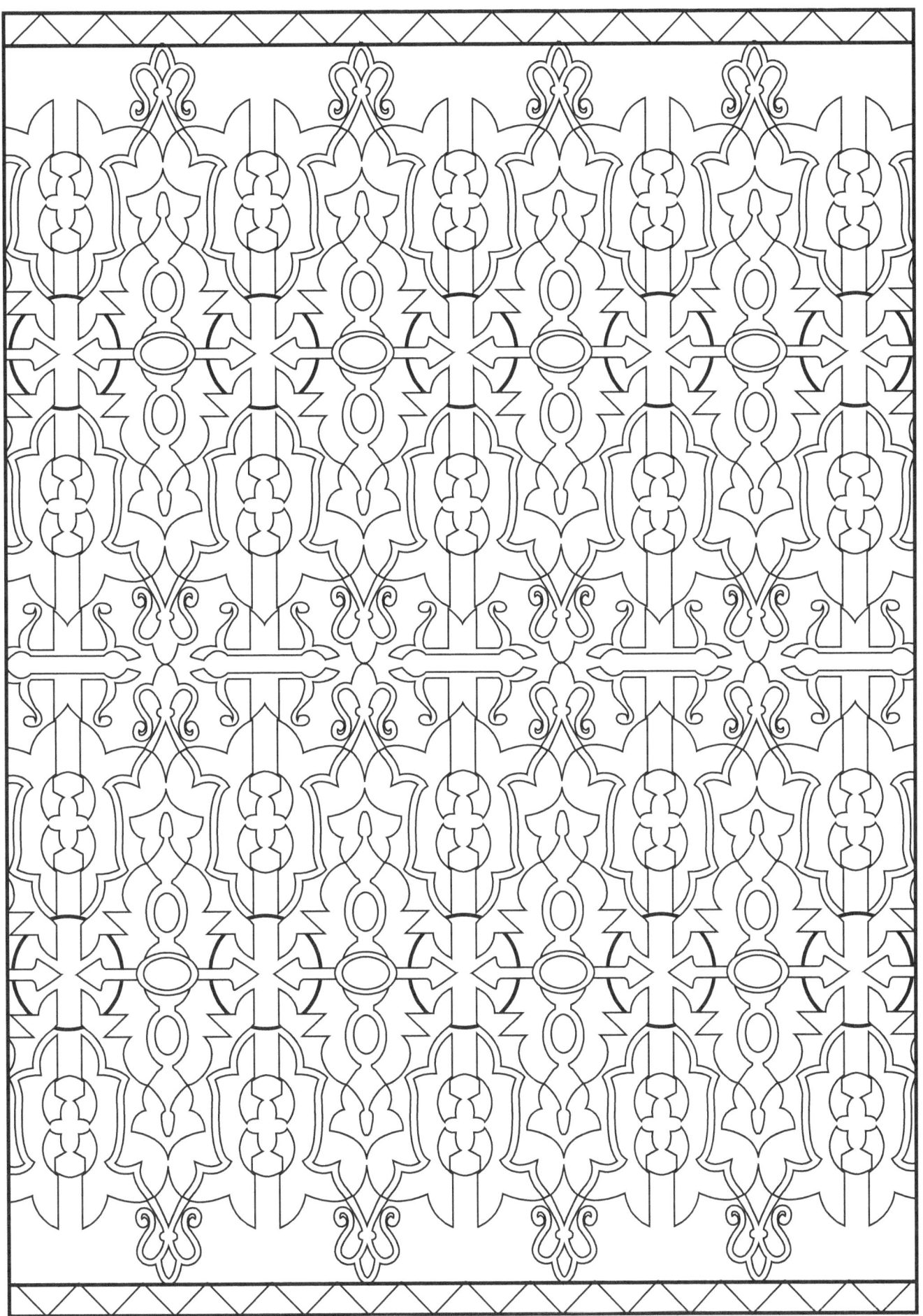

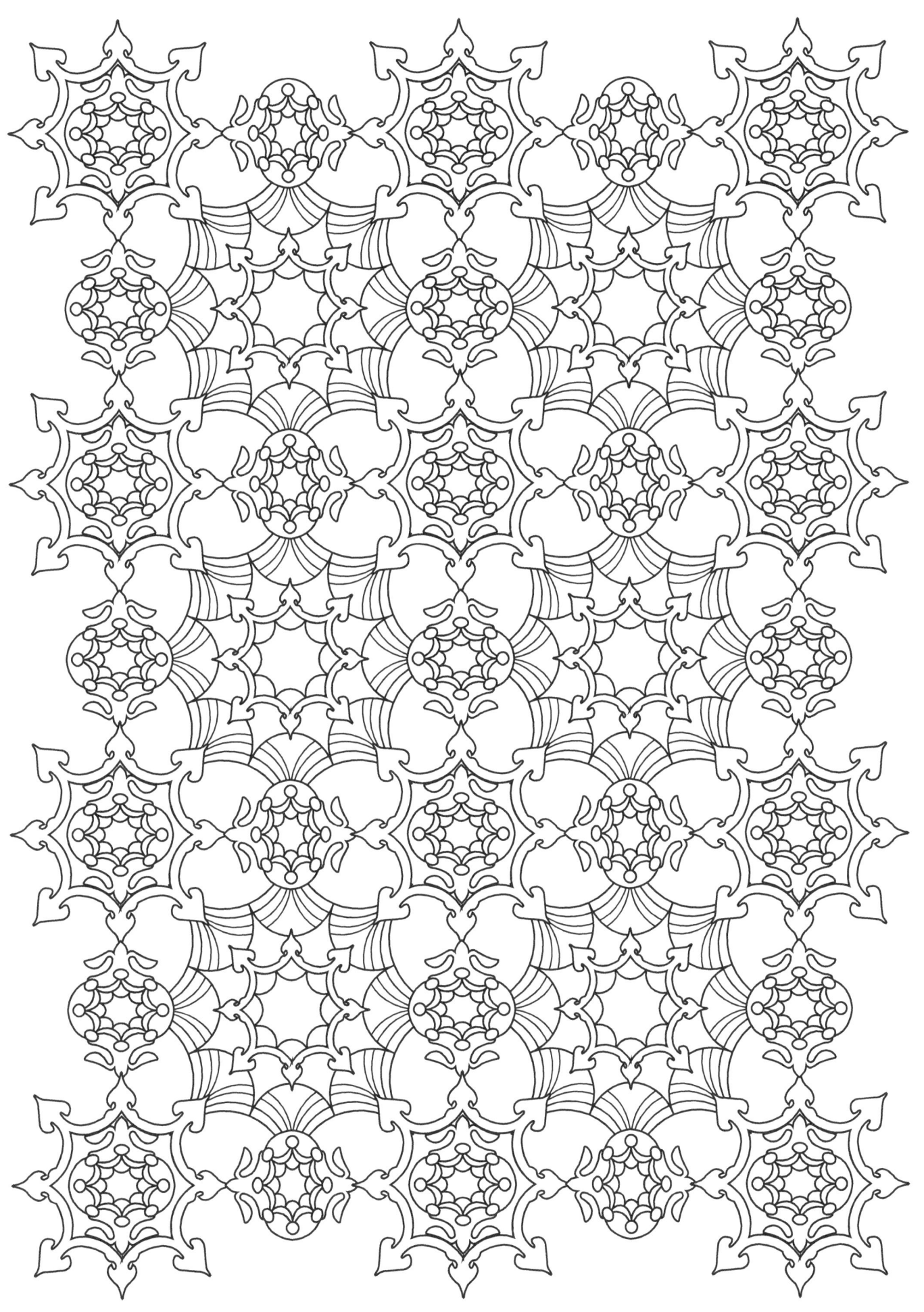

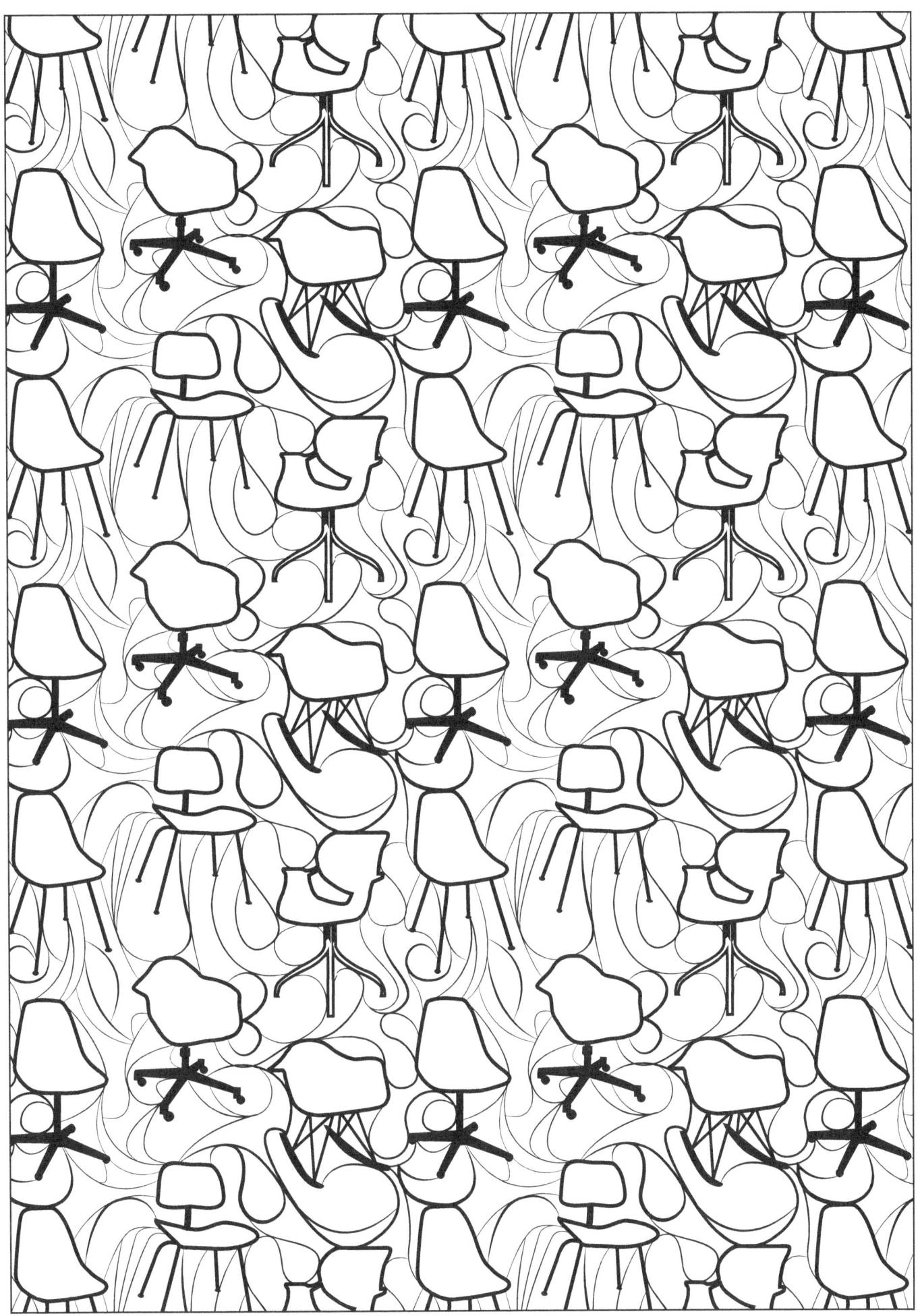

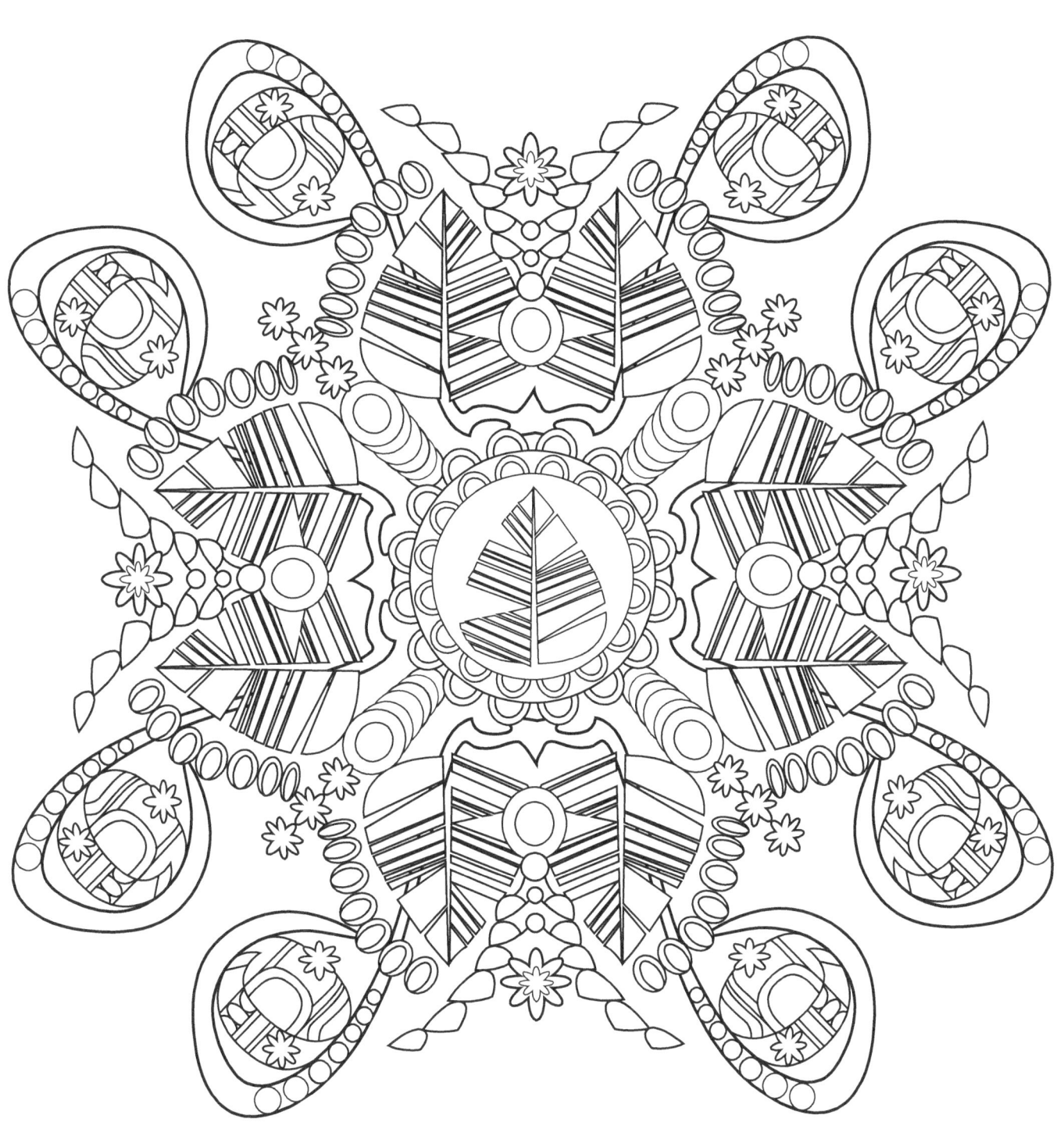

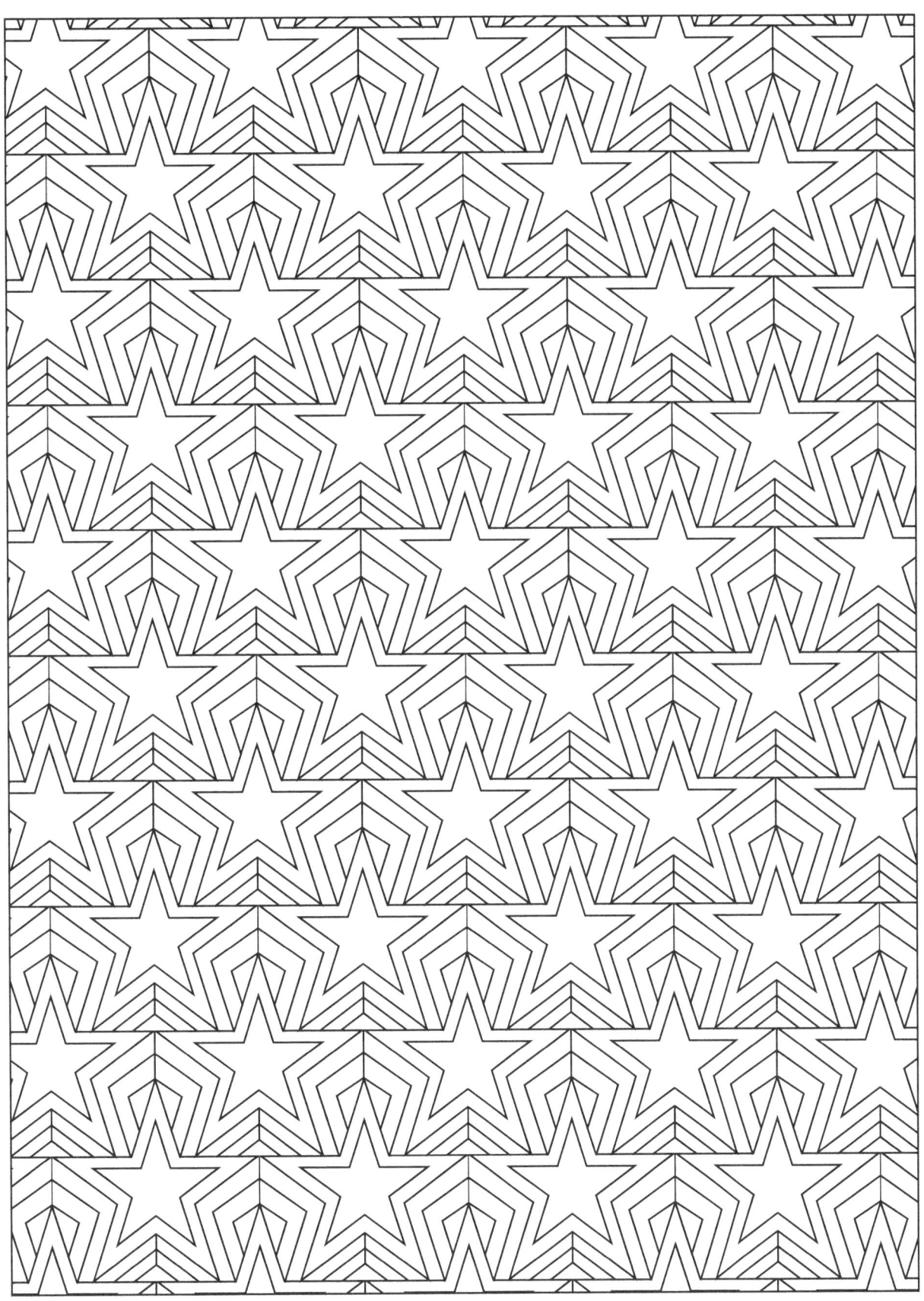

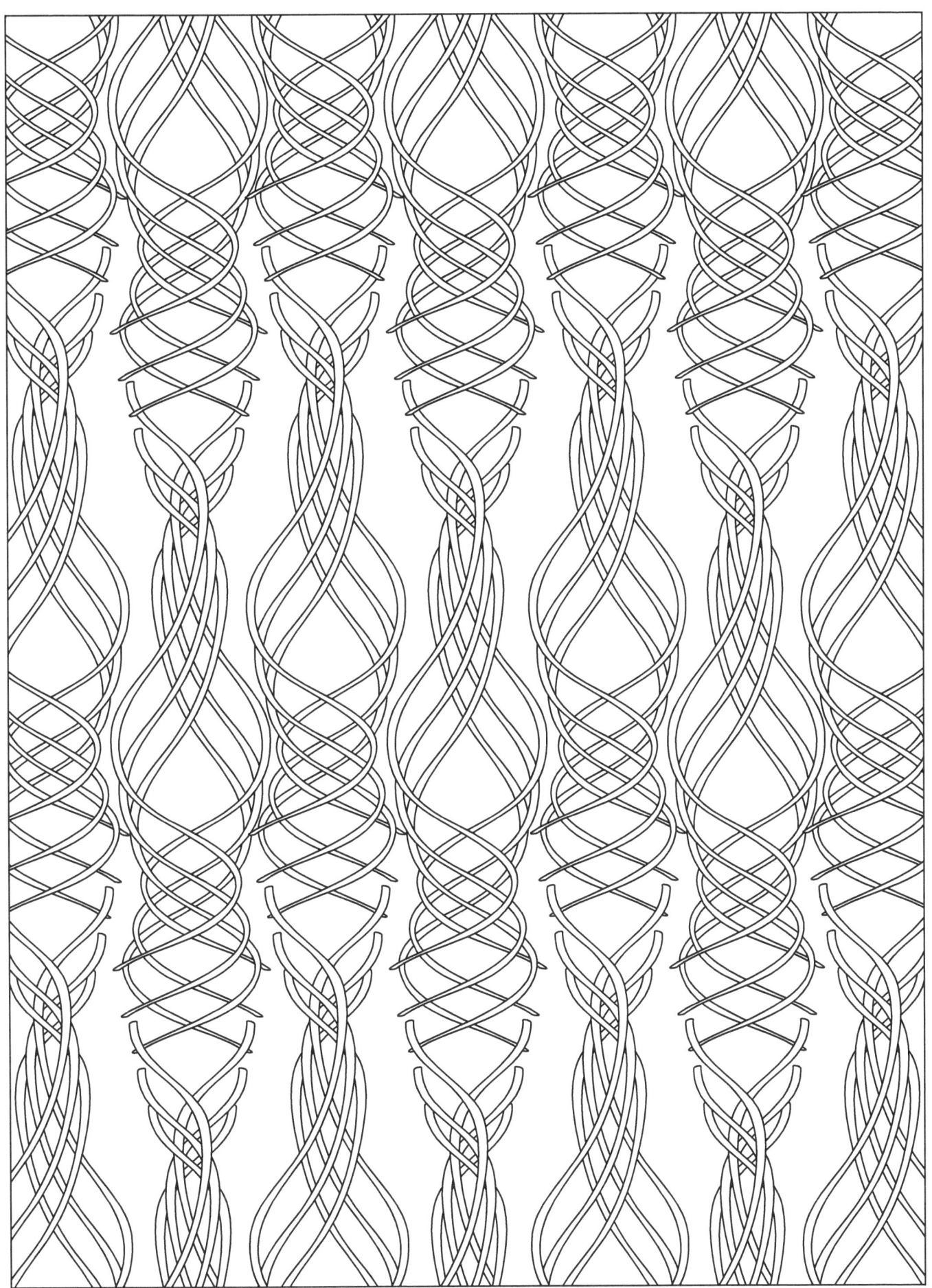

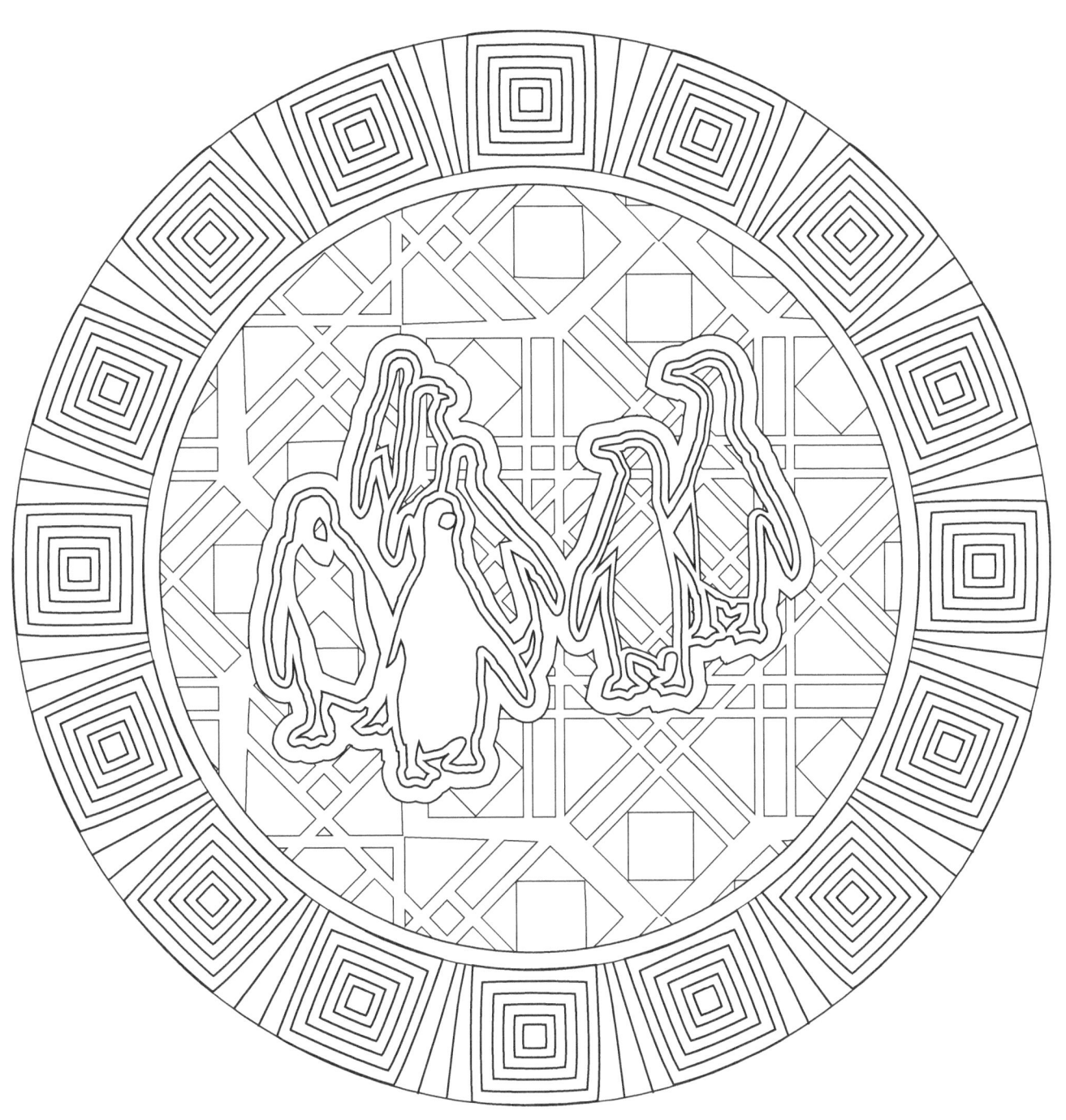

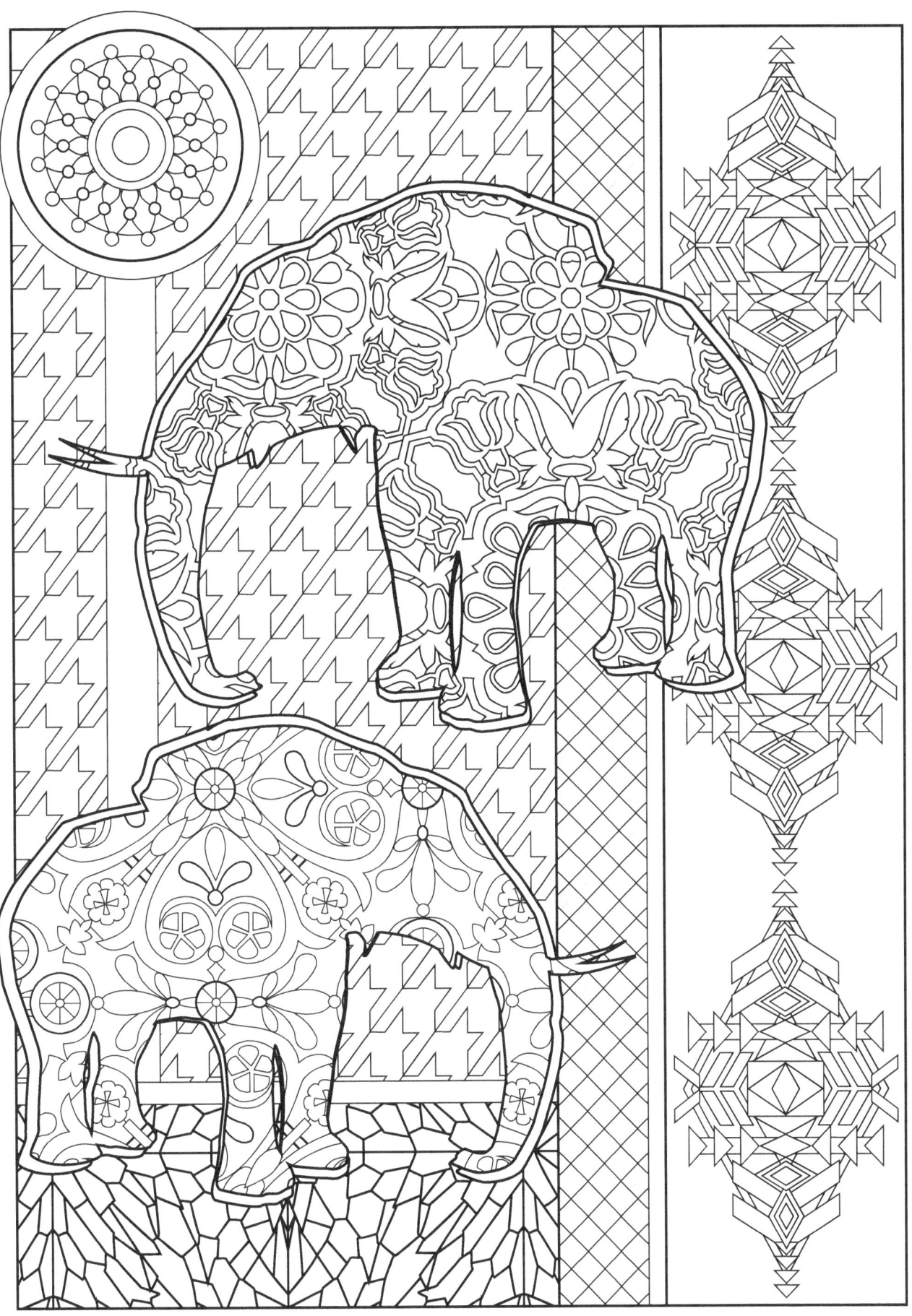

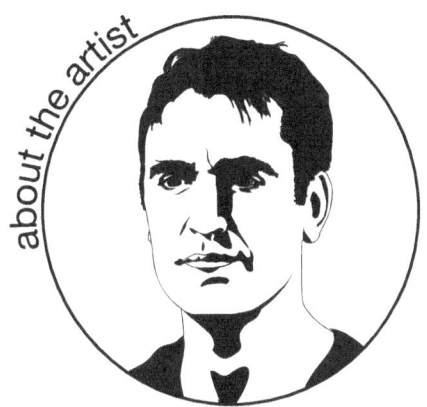

Who: Mark Cesarik

What: Artist & designer in the home, craft and apparel industries. Also a husband, father and lifelong Cleveland sports fan.

Where: New York City

When: est 1970's

Why: Deep-seeded need to doodle and be creative.

about the editor:

Jenean Morrison is the author/artist of many additional coloring books, including the Amazon best-seller *Flower Designs Coloring Book, Volume One*. Her books may be found on Amazon.com and at other retailers internationally.

.